The Bitter Harvest
Church and State in Northern Ireland

for Shirley Ann

Albert J. Menendez

THE BITTER HARVEST

Church and State

in Northern Ireland

Robert B. Luce, Inc.   Washington–New York

Contents

Preface

In a sense, this book began in the summer of 1966 when news reports reached the U.S. that a young Catholic had been murdered, presumably by a terrorist underground group called the Ulster Volunteer Force, in Belfast's Malvern Street. Then there were reports that Protestant-Catholic relations were deteriorating rapidly under the impetus of a militantly aggressive preacher named Ian Paisley. I was fascinated and appalled that religious conflict on such a scale could still exist in a modern western democracy. So I began to collect materials and information from Ulster itself so that I could intelligently appraise the significance of these tragic events.

My interest has intensified through the years since 1966. Despite protestations to the contrary, this is truly the most vivid contemporary example of a religious war, despite very real economic and political factors. Religious conflict, because of its very irrationality and unpredictability, should concern us all because its potential may exist in almost every country.

What I have tried to do in this book is to show how severe religious differences can escalate into antagonism and eventually, civil conflict. I have looked into the specific areas of conflict which divide Protestants and Catholics in Ulster. Since Protestants fear incorporation into a united Ireland, I decided it would be wise to look at church-state relations in the Republic to see if Protestant fears were groundless or reasonable. I have also chosen to survey the American participation in Ulster, since there has been a considerable degree of American involvement on both sides of the struggle.

I have reproduced some authentic material from Ulster, which deals with the religious aspect of the conflict. This, I believe, will add much local flavor and will indicate the intensity of the struggle. Most of the documents reproduced are from the Protestant side because they are the ones who most frequently discuss the religious dimensions. I have tried to be as fair and objective as possible, though my abhorrence of religious fanaticism and bigotry will become clear to readers.

I suppose that no American can truly understand Ireland. We can only attempt an explanation in light of our experiences and biases. I cannot claim complete objectivity. I am committed to the principle of the separation of church and state. I believe that complete religious liberty for all should be guaranteed by law. The state should be neutral regarding religion, should guarantee free exercise of religious belief and practice, should never become an instrumentality of discrimination and should never subsidize sectarian institutions. Though Americans have no right to arrogantly suggest that another nation adopt their system of government or laws. I suggest that a true separation of the fundamental processes of church and state would be a desirable objective for both Ulster and the Irish Republic.

The events depicted in this book offer some sobering lessons for Americans and indeed for all humanity. The use of the state to promote certain religious goals and values is deplorable. The "excessive entanglements" between church and state in both Irelands, in education, housing policy, employment opportunities and a host of other areas are dangerous to community peace and harmony. The arbitrary policy of keeping children apart solely on religious grounds is tragic. The recent outbreak of religious violence is a grim reminder of one society's failure to solve the age-old problem of interlocking the two swords of church and state.

8

One word of explanation. I have used "Ulster" and "Northern Ireland" interchangeably, though Ulster historically refers to a nine-county province, three of which, Monaghan, Cavan, and Donegal, are within the Irish Republic. Northern Ireland was the name devised by the British when the United Kingdom of Great Britain and Northern Ireland came into existence in 1921.

My appreciation for assistance in this book project goes to many people. I would especially like to thank my two "bosses" Glenn L. Archer and C. Stanley Lowell for their encouragement and support, and my colleague Edd Doerr for publishing my Ireland articles in *Church & State*. I would also like to thank the following: Mr. David de Boinville of the British Embassy in Washington; the Northern Ireland Industrial Development Office in New York; the Northern Ireland government and its Ministry of Education; Rev. Martin Smyth, Grand Master of the Orange Order; and many individuals in Belfast, whose names must remain anonymous.

A special word of appreciation must go to the secretaries who helped put the manuscript together: Pamela Mason, Doris Black, Lorraine Mays, Noemi Funes, Barbara Moon and Jerry Hutson.

Albert J. Menendez
Silver Spring, Maryland
October 31, 1973

✚✚

"THE GLORIOUS TWELFTH"

March together, Orangemen, with loyalty and pride,
Let no hatred mar our union, no enemy divide,
Put away misunderstanding, trust each other heart and soul,
Till the morn of peace is dawning and the clouds asunder roll.

March together, brethren, look to God to guard His own,
He is watching all our movements, His right arm around us
    thrown,
A constant shield from danger, in life's storms He whispers,
    'Peace'.
Trust your cause to God Almighty and the tempest soon will
    cease.

'No Surrender' is our watchword, till the dangers pass away,
Man the walls of truth and freedom, trust in God and watch
    and pray.
Onward in the cause of Ulster; trust in God and plan to do;
The Orange banner floats above us, the same our fathers flew.

From Canada, U.S.A. and Albion, with Scotia's sons so grand,
We extend to you from Ulster an Orangeman's welcoming
    hand.
Never, ever, shall we surrender the glories of our past:
The sword of the Lord and of Gideon will defend us to the
    last.

              Wor. Bro. ROBERT BROWN,
                  Secretary, L.O.L. 762 (No. 1).

✚✚

1.   A Divided Society

> "For too long we have been torn and divided.
> Ours is called a Christian country. We could
> have enriched our politics with our Christianity;
> but far too often we have debased our
> Christianity with our politics."
>
> *Terence O'Neill, Prime Minister*
> *of Northern Ireland 1963-69*

Northern Ireland is a deeply religious country in the
formal sense of church affiliation and participation. The 1961
census figures indicated that 98 percent of Northern Irish
residents identify with a particular religion. There were 900,000
Protestants and 497,000 Roman Catholics in the 1961 survey.
In previous census reports 99 to 99.6 percent of the individuals
indicated a religious preference. Religion was not included in
the 1971 census for Northern Ireland, so today's statistics will
have to be estimated. Northern Ireland is estimated to be 65
percent Protestant and 35 percent Roman Catholic. It is
interesting to note that the Protestant and Catholic percentages
of the population have remained almost stable since the 1911
census. (See Table 1)

The Presbyterian Church is the strongest Protestant
church in Northern Ireland, with close ties to the Church of
Scotland. The second largest Protestant church is the Church

of Ireland, an Evangelical variety of Anglicanism. A number of other Protestant churches, Methodist, Brethren, Congregationalist and a small Unitarian body called "The non-subscribing Presbyterians" have representation in Ulster. One of the fastest growing groups is Ian Paisley's Free Presbyterian Church. (See Table 2)

The religious composition in Ulster has been remarkably stable since the census of 1911. The Roman Catholic population was 34.2 percent in 1911 and 34.9 percent in 1961. Despite a larger Catholic birthrate, a much larger number of Catholics emigrated from Northern Ireland over the last 50 years. As can be noted from Table 2, the religious composition has been relatively stable within all counties except for Londonderry City which has become more heavily Catholic. Geographically the areas east of the Bann River, Belfast City, Antrim and Down are the real Protestant strongholds of Ulster. Areas west of the Bann and bordering the Irish Republic have Catholic majorities. Some smaller towns such as Newry and Strabane have 80 to 90 percent Catholic majorities. When one speaks of Protestant Ulster, one really means the northeastern coast of Ireland with its close proximity to Presbyterian Scotland.

It is possible the Roman Catholic population has increased somewhat during the last decade, as many Protestants fear. All marriages celebrated in Northern Ireland are recorded by place of occurrence. In 1961, 33.3 percent of the marriages were in Roman Catholic churches. In 1970 this figure had risen to 38 percent, which could possible indicate a Catholic population nearing 40 percent. The number of civil marriages increased from 5.3 percent in 1961 to 7.2 percent in 1970. Marriages registered in Protestant churches declined from 61.4 percent in 1961 to 54.8 percent in 1970. Another indication of a possibly growing Catholic percentage of the total population is seen by an analysis of the school statistics. Forty-one percent of all school-age children in 1961 were Roman Catholic, but this figure has risen to almost 48 percent in 1972.

12

Northern Ireland has the highest birthrate in the United Kingdom with 21.1 births per 1000 population compared to 16.0 for England and Wales and 16.8 for Scotland. The Irish Republic has 21.0.

Ulster's estimated population today is 1,527,000. This represents an increase of 102,000 over the 1961 census, which is a rather significant increase. There were an excess of 173,393 births over deaths during the last decade, but 70,842 people left Northern Ireland for other nations. As one can see, out migration is still a significant factor in equalizing the population in the north of Ireland.

Northern Ireland may be referred to as a bi-confessional society since nearly everyone identifies himself as a Catholic or Protestant. The churches are remarkably conservative institutions as they institutionalize values, beliefs and emotions. By teaching the importance of differing doctrines to successive generations, the churches transmit past differences into the present and future.

There is a remarkably high degree of church attendance in Northern Ireland. The number of Roman Catholics who attend mass weekly is probably higher than anywhere else in the entire Catholic world. A 1959 survey at Queens University indicated 94 percent of the Roman Catholics attended church on a typical Sunday. Protestant church attendance is much higher in Northern Ireland than anywhere else in the United Kingdom. Protestant church attendance weekly has been estimated at 45 to 55 percent with the Free Presbyterians, Methodists and Presbyterians showing the highest degree of church attendance. Much social life also tends to revolve around the individual parish church. Ulster has a number of voluntary associations associated with individual religions.

There are differences, of course, in the occupational status of Protestant and Catholic, much of which is due to the significantly higher birth rate. The Catholic birthrate is 28.3 per 1000 live births in Northern Ireland, compared to about 20.0 for Protestants. The average Catholic family contains

13

4.17 individuals compared to 3.08 for Protestants. The latest sociological and demographic survey conducted on a nationwide basis indicates the following class breakdown by religion:

Protestant		*Roman Catholic*
16%	Business-Professional	9%
30%	Lower Middle Class	24%
48%	Working Class	58%
6%	Residual Class	9%

As can be seen Protestants have achieved a higher social status than Roman Catholics. Almost half are in the business-professional or "lower middle class," which corresponds to the American middle class, compared to only one third of Roman Catholics. Protestants also tend to be the larger farmers and they have more skilled laborers than Roman Catholics. A survey conducted in Portadown in 1960 indicated only 13 percent of the Catholics are in the professional-administrative-executive classes compared to 24 percent of Protestants. Similarly 55 percent of Catholics were in semiskilled or un-skilled work compared to 26 percent of Protestants. The combination of historic and economic factors has probably accounted for this, plus the differences in educational attain-ment. It is significant that Protestants also predominate in the upper echelons of the business and professional communities, in the labor unions, and in the Northern Ireland Civil Service. Ninety-four percent of the upper grade civil service positions are held by Protestants. The textile and shipping industries are also heavily Protestant, particularly in the Harlan and Wolff Shipyards where 95 percent of the workers are Protestant. The university teaching staff is heavily Protestant and 88 percent of the Royal Ulster Constabulary was Protestant in 1970. Catholics, however, do relatively better in those positions under the direct control of London. For example, 57 percent of postal workers are Catholic. (There has always been a large Catholic participation in the legal profession, and the first Lord Chief Justice of Northern Ireland was a Catholic.)

As the whole world now knows, Northern Ireland is a land divided along religious lines. That seemingly irreconcilable division affects virtually every area of society. Ulster is probably the world's most rigorously divided society in terms of religion—even more so than Holland, Germany, Switzerland, the Indian subcontinent or the southern islands of the Philippines. What astounds many observers is the virulence and permanence of the religious divisions.

The most extraordinary evidence of this separation is the housing patterns in Ulster, especially in Belfast. It seems bizarre in the extreme to know a person's religion by his street address but Belfast's neighborhoods are deeply segregated by religion. Even many of the smaller side streets are delineated by religious affiliations. Mobs of the opposing religion have often invaded "hostile" streets, intimidating the inhabitants and forcibly relocating them in "their own" side of town. Though rigidity in housing was beginning to break down somewhat in the early and mid-60s, the recent troubles have hardened the segregation. Thousands have been driven from mixed neighborhoods. During 1972-73 thousands of Catholics and Protestants were forced to leave neighborhoods where they were a minority. Most were Catholics living in predominantly Protestant areas. *Time* commented on March 5, 1973—

The Protestant and Catholic communities have grown farther apart than ever, physically as well as ideologically. A still secret housing study of Belfast reveals that a large-scale population shift within the troubled city has taken place during the past two years. As of 1971, about 25 percent of the people in public housing projects lived in mixed areas; today virtually none do. More than 10,000 families have moved since 1969, half within the past year alone; about 80% are Catholics who have taken refuge in deteriorating West

15

Belfast, which is fast becoming the city's single, sprawling Catholic ghetto.

In trying to explore how such segregation could have occurred in housing areas, I asked a number of Belfast natives, including Canon Michael Hamilton of Washington's National Cathedral (Episcopal). All agreed that it had occurred rather informally at first—due to the desire of the people to live among "their own." It was a longing for security which reflected already deep religious divisions. Both sides generally accepted the arrangement and each succeeding generation fostered and maintained the housing segregation. The deep political and cultural chasm enforced it. After Ulster's formal incorporation into the United Kingdom in 1921, the Housing Authorities, which built and maintained the public housing sector, reinforced the traditions by segregating Catholics and Protestants into their own "estates." Only limited housing integration ensued and those were restricted to middle or upper middle-class areas. There is also "informal" pressure on landlords to sell only to their co-religionists.

One must remember, of course, that Catholics and Protestants have been antagonists, in a political and social as well as theological sense, in Ulster since the Scotch-Irish "plantation" of the early 17th century. The sense of separation has been reinforced by the memories of the massacre of Protestants in 1641, of Catholics under Cromwell in 1649, the Battle of the Boyne in 1690, the revolutions of the 1790s, the Evangelical Revival of 1859, and the sporadic communal outbursts since 1886. The two communities have lived in two different worlds for so long that what appears to be frightful division to outsiders is regarded as natural to the participants.

Religious separation is found in innumerable instances. The most serious is the almost total separation in the educational systes of the province. I shall deal with this issue more fully in a later chapter, but, suffice it to say, that the Roman Catholic Church's insistence on separate school systems (called "voluntary" schools) has made it impossible for Prot-

16

estant and Catholic children to come to know each other or to understand each other's viewpoint. Playgrounds and school activities are separate. The structure and orientation of the curriculum are quite divergent, as the state schools emphasize English history and culture while Roman Catholic schools glorify the Irish heritage and language with great fervor.

The treatment accorded religion in the schools is vastly different. The Catholic demand for parochial education has, perforce, created a state system that is, in effect, all Protestant. Only a tiny handful of Catholics violates the Canon Law on Education.

Even recreational and reading tastes vary. Protestants read the *Belfast News Letter,* while Catholics read the *Irish News.* (See insert) Protestants prefer the BBC; Catholics watch Irish Television from Dublin. One wag has suggested that Catholic and Protestant neighborhoods can be discerned from the sky by looking at the shape of television cables! (H for the BBC, straight for Irish TV.) Both communities read their own ecclesiastical publications, wherein suspicion and intergroup tensions are often reinforced. In athletics, certain games are reserved for Protestants, such as rugby, cricket, and bowling. Gaelic football, hurling, and boxing are largely Catholic.

Occupational relations are somewhat better, as Protestants and Catholics generally work together with a minimum of social tensions (except around the Protestant marching season, the 12th of July, when friendships become strained). Catholics are under-represented in the professional-technical class and over-represented in the semiskilled and unskilled labor class. The trade unions, representing some 250,000 workers, have generally been a nonsectarian force. Most unions are religiously integrated, and communal relations have been relatively stable in the shipbuilding and aircraft industries despite the recent violence. The Northern Ireland Committee of the Irish Congress of Trade Unions attempted to discourage sectarian outbursts and passed the following resolution in May 1960.

Irish News, Wed., 15th August

LENADOON CATHOLICS ATTACKED

Catholic residents of the big Lenadoon housing estate on the outskirts of Belfast fought hand-to-hand battle last night with Protestant extremist mobs who invaded the area in an attempt to burn people out of their homes. The attackers—armed with cudgels and bottles and many carrying pistols—swarmed into the estate from the Suffolk district. They were spotted by two women who raised the alarm. A warning siren was sounded and brought hundreds of residents onto the streets. In the initial attack, involving a 40-strong mob, windows in houses in Doon Road and Horn Drive were smashed. At least two shots were fired.

The Newsletter, Wed., 15th Aug.

Terror after invasion by RC bonfire mob

PROTESTANTS FLEE LENADOON HOMES

Protestants fled their homes in Belfast's Suffolk area last night when it was invaded by up to 500 Roman Catholics. The trouble started about 11 p.m. following an eve of August 15 bonfire in the Lenadoon Avenue area. There were conflicting reports of what happened. Residents maintained that the invaders smashed the windows of Protestant homes and that Protestants who gathered to protect their families came under attack. An Army spokesman said 100 Roman Catholics came down from the top of Lenadoon estate and troops drove a wedge between them and 50 Protestants at Lenadoon Avenue-Stewartstown Road.

18

This Conference declares its opposition to all forms of discrimination on the basis of race, religion, sex, color or politics, as such discrimination or segregation leads to strife and often loss of life. The Conference calls upon all Trade Unionists to oppose discrimination wherever it may raise its head and to practice tolerance, equality, and justice.

Ulster's political parties are sectarian in nature. Primarily because of fundamental disagreements concerning the nature of the Ulster state, disagreements which are historically coterminous with religion, the parties draw their constituency from only one religion. Ulster is one of the very few countries in the world where economic and class differentiation do not determine the outcome of elections. Working class Protestants have voted against their own economic self-interest for 50 years because of religious allegiance. Even the Labour Party, the historic defender of working class interests, is divided into the Northern Ireland Labour Party (primarily Protestant) and Republican Labour (Catholic). Nonsectarian, liberally oriented parties are suspect in the highly charged sectarian environment.

Politics in Northern Ireland are more highly fragmented and balkanized than ever. There are at least eight major political groupings ranging from left to right of the political spectrum. On the Protestant side, the official Unionists are still the strongest party, led by former Prime Minister Brian Faulkner. They swept 41 percent of the local government elections in May 1973 and will undoubtedly remain the strongest party in Ulster, though they have lost strength from previous years. They are somewhat to the right of the center. They have urged "peace, order, and good government" but are pretty much a status quo party that would like to keep things as they are. The party is primarily middle class and some upper class but has always received a large working class vote. The party is almost completely Protestant with only a handful of Catholic supporters.

As I will point out there was a crucial time in Ulster's

history when many Catholics would have been willing to support the Unionist Party, but the intolerance and shortsighted stupidity of Unionist leaders prevented them from broadening their base. Today, of course, their base is narrower than ever. The Unionists are relatively conservative economically and are moving in the direction of integrated education. They have accepted many of the changes in the last few years such as a charter of human rights and a community relations commission. They still demand control over the police force of Northern Ireland (which is now under the control of London). There are a number of "unofficial Unionists," mostly right wing individuals. They will vote with the Unionists and of course are strongly loyal to Ulster's traditional setup and would like to return Ulster to the way that it was a decade ago and forget what has happened in the past few years.

The main policy of the Democratic Unionist Party (DUP), founded by Ian Paisley and formerly called the Protestant Unionist Party, is to maintain the Protestant supremacy; it favors total integration of Ulster into the United Kingdom. Paisley's party would prefer Ulster to be treated as Scotland and Wales are, with only a minimum of autonomy. This is a new position in some respects since Paisley was always a militant Ulster separatist, but now he and his party feel that Protestant rights can be guaranteed only if Ulster is integrated into the mother country. During the recent campaign, however, Paisley has played down some of his total integration policy. This party is generally working class and is more liberal than the Unionists on economic issues.

Paisley's supporters feel that they have not gotten a fair break from the Unionist government in recent years. Much of Paisley's support has been drifting away in the past year to the VUPP (Vanguard Unionist Progressive Party) led by militant right-winger William Craig. Together the Vanguard and the Democratic Unionists pulled 14 percent of the vote in the local elections in May and it was only because of the individualism and fragmentation of Ulster that these two groups are fighting

20

separate election campaigns. They are basically the extreme right wing of Ulster politics and could be united. However, Craig's Vanguard Party is even further to the right of Paisley on many issues: it is rather populist and almost fascist in many respects. It has endorsed an independent dominion of Ulster, something like Rhodesia. Though this policy was favored by only 4 percent of the people in the recent *Fortnight* poll, the Vanguard party received a considerable vote in certain areas.

Its radical extremism comes through in some of its policy statements. For example, it wants a trimming down of the universities, which it denounces as centers of special privilege. This seems absurd to this observer, because Ulster actually has a very tiny percentage of college-educated people—one of the lowest in the western world. This is rank anti-intellectualism. The Vanguard is also obsessed by allegedly biased news coverage from Britain and plans a new Ulster state television broadcasting authority to "advance the Ulster identity." The Vanguard movement is probably receiving quite a bit of support from Protestant groups such as the UDA and the UVF. The Vanguard and the Paisleyites constitute a "loyalist coalition" pledged to obstruct the new government.

Only two parties are generally nonsectarian, the Alliance Party and the Northern Ireland Labour Party. The Alliance Party genuinely affirms a belief in a new Ulster where Protestants and Catholics will work together. Their two leaders are Protestant Bob Cooper, who ran for a seat in Catholic West Belfast and Oliver Napier, a Catholic who stood as the Alliance candidate in Protestant East Belfast. Both are courageous men and seem to have qualities of leadership. Unfortunately, the polarization between religions has worsened over the last year and the Alliance Party is receiving much less support than many had hoped. It is receiving much more Catholic support than Protestant support, which indicates the hardening of Protestant attitudes.

The *Belfast Telegraph,* Ulster's best newspaper, has endorsed the Alliance Party, but they only pulled 14 percent of

21

the vote in the local government elections in May. They are basically a moderate middle-class party which opposes both internment and terrorism. Their main support comes from the more affluent and better educated. Many of their candidates were viciously attacked by sectarian extremists during the recent campaign for the new regional assembly.

The Northern Ireland Labour Party, moderately socialist and pro-border, is the weakest party in the Ulster elections, having pulled only 3 percent of the local government election vote. This party is affiliated with the British Labour party and actually pulled about 15 percent in the Westminster general election in 1970. However, more people vote Labour in the general election rather than for their local assembly election because the Labour Party is the main opposition party to the conservative Unionists. However, the future of the NILP seems bleak indeed because of the polarization of the country and the fact that those Protestants and Catholics who want to build a new Ulster are working in the Alliance Party.

There are two major parties on the Catholic side. The SDLP, or Social Democratic Labour Party, is the main Catholic middle-class party, though it also has much working class support. It is a little left of center and is the main exponent of the official Catholic viewpoint, though many Catholic moderates are supporting the Alliance Party. Gerry Fitt represents West Belfast in the Westminster Parliament in London and is the main leader of the SDLP. SDLP favors eventual reunification with the Republic of Ireland, which precludes any significant Protestant support for them. They favor the ending of internment and an amnesty for all prisoners, the repeal of the Flags and Emblems Act (which will allow Catholics to fly the Irish flag), a strong anti-discrimination body within the government to protect Catholics, reform of the police and a charter of rights. They are trying to encourage more Catholic participation in the police forces. They also favor more public housing and government spending for economic problems. The SDLP polled 14 percent in the recent local elections.

The most left-wing party on the Catholic side is the Republican Party. This party favors a United Ireland. The Republicans are considered radically socialist and favor nationalization of industry in Ulster. They have most of their support among poor working class Catholics in West Ulster and in parts of West Belfast. Surprising to those of us who do not support reunification with Ireland, the Republicans do have the best position of any party on education. They have endorsed comprehensive integrated education and the secularization of the educational system in Ulster for which they deserve a great deal of credit. They pulled 7 percent in the local government elections.

A number of Catholics, of course, have boycotted the Assembly elections because they favor the provisional IRA's violent solution to Ulster's problems. They want unity with the Republic of Ireland at all costs. Perhaps in retrospect, it would have been wiser for the government to have allowed the IRA's political arm, the Sinn Fein Party, to field candidates for the election. This would at least allow the government to know the true extent of their support, rather than having to estimate it. It would also help to ventilate some of the anger felt in the Catholic community. The *Fortnight* poll published in May 1973 indicated that 6 percent of Roman Catholics favored the official IRA and 8 percent favored the provisional IRA. This is a significant 14 percent who may have boycotted the election and continued to support terrorism and violence.

The local elections in May were disappointing to those who hoped for reconciliation and peace, though 70 percent voted, a very impressive turnout for a local election. The old sectarian alliances were maintained. People still voted for the Orange and the Green. The discredited Unionists won a large, but declining, percentage of the Protestant vote. Most Catholics voted for the SDLP. The Alliance Party ran far behind its

23

original predictions. Fifty-five percent of the total vote went for various Unionist parties and only 17 percent voted for the two nonsectarian moderate parties. Nine percent voted for other independent and generally extreme candidates, particularly in Protestant areas.

The results of the June Assembly elections were disappointing in one respect but encouraging in another. Sectarianism and traditional voting tended to predominate. The Alliance Party secured only eight of the seventy eight seats and Northern Ireland Labour, only one. Twenty-three "official" Unionists were elected, and a surprising twelve "unofficial anti-White Paper" Unionists won seats. All are Protestants. Nineteen members of the predominantly Catholic SDLP were elected. One SDLP member is a controversial Protestant, Ivan Cooper, who represents the mostly Catholic constituency of Mid-Derry. Cooper was a leader of the Civil Rights Movement and is a liberal Protestant. The SDLP swept the Catholic areas, leaving Republicans and others without any seats. Only 2 percent of the votes were "spoiled," as the provisional IRA had encouraged. This shows their declining support. The overall turnout was an encouraging 72 percent. The extreme Protestant militants won 15 seats, 8 for the Paisleyite DUP and 7 for the Vanguard.

On the all-important issue of whether the new Assembly can really govern Ulster, it appears that 51 of the 78 winners are pledged to support the White Paper compromises for "power-sharing" between Protestants and Catholics. Twenty-seven are opposed and may prove to be an obstructionist force.

The first meeting of the Assembly in the late summer of 1973 was disrupted by the Craig-Paisley "loyalists" and disbanded after one day. British impatience with Ulster and the rising demand for bringing the boys home may lead to some serious political decisions in the coming months. Prime Minister Heath made known his displeasure during a two-day visit to Belfast in August. The future of Ulster's political governability is progressively growing bleaker.

24

An historic agreement signed on November 22, 1973 may be the most hopeful sign for Ulster in years. The new executive will be a coalition of 6 Protestant Unionists, 4 Catholic SDLP men and 1 from the nonsectarian Alliance Party. The Chief Executive will be Protestant Brian Faulkner and the Deputy Chief Executive, Gerry Fitt, a Catholic. It remains to be seen whether the fanatics led by Ian Paisley and William Craig will wreck the new coalition government, as they have threatened. If so, the responsibility for further violence must rest on their shoulders.

To understand the turbulent present, it is instructive to look at Ulster's history.

Table 1

The Religious Composition of Ulster, 1911 and 1961

County	Protestants				Catholics			
	1911		1961		1911		1961	
	Number 000s	%	Number 000s	%	Number 000s	%	Number 000s	%
Belfast	293	75.9	302	72.6	93	24.1	114	27.4
Antrim	154	79.8	207	75.5	39	20.2	67	24.5
Down	140	68.6	191	71.5	64	31.4	76	28.5
Armagh	66	55.0	62	52.5	54	45.0	56	47.5
Londonderry-City	18	43.9	18	33.3	23	56.1	36	66.7
County	58	58.6	64	57.1	41	41.4	48	42.9
Fermanagh	27	44.3	24	47.1	34	55.7	27	52.9
Tyrone	63	44.4	61	45.5	79	55.6	73	54.5
Total 6 counties	819	65.7	929	65.1	427	34.2	497	34.9

Table 2

Religious Preferences in Ulster	1961	%	Change since 1951
Roman Catholic	497,547	34.9	+ 26,087
Presbyterian	413,113	29.0	+ 2,898
Church of Ireland	344,800	24.2	− 8,445
Methodist	71,865	5.0	+ 5,226
Brethren	16,847	1.2	− 998
Baptist	13,765	1.0	+ 1,895
Congregational	9,838	0.7	+ 492
Unitarian	5,613	0.4	− 660
Others (Free Presbyterian)	23,236	1.6	+ 5,802
Not stated	28,418	2.0	+ 22,553

2.   The Burden of History

The history of Ireland is a story of turbulence, drama, heros, traitors, broken promises, and long unfullfilled dreams. Let us briefly recall some of the highlights of religious history, church-state problems, and interfaith conflict which have shaped the way Protestants and Catholics view each other in Ulster today.

Religion, like it or not, has played a central role in the history of Ireland. The burden of historical memory hangs over Ulster today like a pall. Those shortsighted modern historians who reject the significant role that religion has played in the history of western civilization are making a big mistake. Especially in relation to Ireland, deeply held religious beliefs have altered and shaped the outcome of many events. There would be no separate Ulster today had it not been for religion. Home rule for Ireland would not have been delayed for so long except for religious antagonisms. Religious conflict brought forth the Glorious Revolution, the Williamite Settlement and the penal laws. Religion has been used to keep poor Protestants and Catholics apart. If it were not for religion, Ireland would probably be one nation today. There's a line in the lively Orange song "Sandy Row" which, in speaking of the Battle of the Boyne, says, "it seems like only yesterday to the folks of Sandy Row." This is one of the problems of interfaith relations in Ulster today. There's too much of yesterday and too little of tomorrow.

27

The Reformation and post-Reformation periods were fraught with political and religious interaction. Since Ireland remained loyal to the Catholic church, this posed special political problems to the Crown. Hence, since Protestantism was equated with loyalty, the famous attempt to "plant" the northeastern province of Ireland, called Ulster, with Scottish and English Protestant settlers began in 1609. Economic considerations were prominent in this policy.

It wasn't long before antagonisms erupted into violence. There was a fearful massacre of the Protestant settlers by Catholic natives in 1641, followed by Oliver Cromwell's brutal retaliatory massacres of 1649. Ireland became a battleground over control of the English Crown. The attempt to recover England for Catholicism by King James II in the 1680s led to the famous revolt of the Protestants, who rallied around William of Orange, a Dutch Calvinist and his wife, Mary. Protestant victories at the siege of Derry in 1689 and the battle on the "green grasy slopes of the Boyne" in 1690 solidified the Protestant ascendancy.

Intensely discriminatory penal laws were enforced against Catholics until 1793. They were reduced to chattel status. This inhumane policy, in addition to its intrinsic immorality, was a catastrophic blunder to the Protestant cause because it strengthened Catholic loyalty to their faith. Catholicism became synonomous with "Irishness" and the church was identified with the cause of Irish freedom and independence. It is interesting to reflect that those areas where the Catholic Church has maintained considerable strength are those countries where it was identified with the national aspirations: Ireland, Poland, and Belgium for example. In countries like Italy, Spain, and Austria, the church was regarded as an oppressive obstruction for centuries, especially by the working classes. It has largely lost the masses in those lands.

In 1798 many Presbyterians and Catholics formed the Society of United Irishmen and fought an abortive rebellion against the Crown. Though they lost, and an official act of union between Ireland and Great Britain went into effect in 1801, the incident indicated the possibility of Protestant and Catholic collaboration.

Those Protestants who opposed complete Catholic emancipation rallied to the newly founded Orange Order in the early 1800s. Liberal-conservative battles split the Presbyterian church in the 1820s and 1830s, as liberals, led by Henry Montgomery formed the non-subscribing Presbyterian church (because they refused to subscribe to the Westminster Confession of Faith). Interestingly, Catholic-Protestant relations were quite friendly in Belfast, at that time regarded as a liberal stronghold. When the first Catholic church, St. Mary's in Chapel Lane, was built in 1784, Protestants generously contributed to the building fund. The Anglican vicar even paid for the pulpit! Protestants attended the dedication ceremony. This friendliness continued until an upsurge of bigotry in the 1850s.

As the Catholic population grew and economic problems increased, so did interfaith tensions. A small riot broke out in Belfast in 1835. A triumvirate of Protestant militants, Dr. Henry Cooke, Rev. Thomas Drew, and Rev. Hugh "Roaring" Hanna, began to foment bitter attacks on the Roman Catholic Church. They promoted "the Second Reformation", an attempt to convert Catholics, and the famous Evangelical Revival of 1859. Invariably, these events led to sectarian riots, beginning in 1857 and continuing spasmodically throughout the century. Interfaith relations have gone downhill ever since this unfortunate period. Religion and politics became more enmeshed than ever. The country was being divided into sullen sectarian enclaves. The newly developed "national school system" was divided almost from the outset on religious lines, contributing further still to the gulf.

Agitation over Ireland's political status, Home Rule or continued Union with Britain, further divided Protestants and Catholics. In 1886 Lord Randolph Churchill discovered the "Orange Card" and stumped Ulster, warning that Home Rule was Rome Rule. Protestants rallied to the cause.

From 1886 to 1912, Protestants and Catholics drew further apart politically. In 1912 this Solemn Covenant pledging resistance to Home Rule at *all* costs was signed by almost 447,000 of the 500,000 adult Protestants in Ulster:

Being convinced in our conscience that Home Rule would be disastrous to the material well-being of Ulster as well as the whole of Ireland, subversive of our civil and religious freedom, destructive of our citizenship, and perilous to the unity of the Empire, we, whose names are underwritten, men of Ulster, loyal subjects of His Gracious Majesty King George V, humbly relying on God whom our fathers in days of stress and trial confidently trusted, do hereby pledge ourselves in solemn Covenant throughout this time of threatened calamity to stand by one another in defending for ourselves and our children our cherished position of equal citizenship in the United Kingdom, and in using all means which may be found necessary to defeat the present conspiracy to set up a Home Rule Parliament in Ireland. And in the event of such a Parliament being forced on us, we solemnly and mutually pledge ourselves to refuse to recognize its authority.

It was too late. Home rule finally passed Parliament, but was postponed by the outbreak of the Guns of August, 1914.

After the war, Ireland was plunged into rebellion and war (inaugurated by the unsuccessful Easter Rising of 1916). As a compromise, demanded by Protestants who feared the consequences of their absorption into a united Ireland, Britain absorbed the six counties of Ulster into the United Kingdom of Great Britain and Northern Ireland, while allowing the Irish Free State (the 26 counties) to go its own way. Partition never really satisfied either side. The boundary was artificially gerrymandered. The historic nine county province of Ulster was sundered, because Protestants feared too close a division (55-45 percent Protestant) to govern effectively. By removing Cavan, Monaghan and Donegal the Protestants had a comfortable 66 percent majority. The Irish coalition government (Fine Gael) accepted the partition reluctantly but bitter diehards (the Fianna Fail) and the Irish Republican Army refused to accept partition and plunged Ireland into a bloody Civil war. "A mounting crescendo of sectarian violence" (in Liam de Paor's phrase) erupted in Belfast in 1921-22. Finally, the pattern of separate Orange and Green states was developed in Ulster. Protestants set about consolidating their power and insuring effective control over the government of "their" province. Catholics in Ulster grudgingly acquiesced but dedicated their efforts to work for eventual reunion. (Actually, Ireland has never been "one" country in the sense that romantics dream of). In 1925, a tripartite agreement on the border question was signed by Great Britain, Ireland and Ulster.

Because of the constant fear of sedition, the Special Powers Act was passed in 1922 and a strong Ulster police force, the Royal Ulster Constabulary, was established. An informal para-military group, the "B-Specials" were organized to preserve the state from internal disruption. Unionists gerrymandered the political system to insure their permanent control.

Ulster was fervently loyal to the war effort against Nazi Germany. Many of Britain's leading generals were Ulstermen and allied military forces were stationed in Ulster during the war. The Irish Republic, however, was neutral in the extreme and refused any support, however peripheral or indirect, to the Allies. This left a sour taste between Ulstermen and the Republic.

One of the cruel ironies of the present turmoil is that Catholic-Protestant relations were generally improving in Ulster through the 1950s and early 1960s. The rise of a Catholic middle class and increasing contacts between Protestant and Catholic professional people were gradually helping to break down barriers. Queens University made overtures to Catholic students. As far back as 1909, for example, a department of scholastic philosophy was established. Then the Catholic-operated Mater hospital was recognized as a teaching hospital,

31

and a professor of Celtic studies was added to the staff. By 1960, 22 percent of the student body was Catholic. The Belfast city hall flew the flag at half-staff when Pope John died in 1963. Changes were appearing everywhere. When the *National Geographic* did a beautiful story on Northern Ireland in the summer of 1964, religious differences were hardly mentioned!

Why did violence erupt now? Perhaps de Tocqueville was right when he observed over one hundred years ago that revolutions don't occur until the possibility of changing the situation becomes realistic. When there is despair, there is usually sullen acceptance; but, when changes occur, a new horizon is opened for those who feel oppressed. They then demand the fullness of the desired changes immediately. This seems to be the pattern of social revolutions.

When Captain Terence O'Neill became Prime Minister in 1963, one could sense the dawn of a new day for Ulster. Though cautious and pragmatic, O'Neill recognized that inequities existed. He recognized that the winds of change were beginning to caress the Irish Republic, too. Hence, the famous meeting between O'Neill and Prime Minister Sean Lemass of the Republic in January, 1965. O'Neill pursued conciliatory policies toward the Catholics and attempted to convince them that they were appreciated and could play a role in the new Ulster. He was determined to improve housing, employment, and local government franchise for the minority. His problem was in dealing with the recalcitrant right-wing Unionists who were content with things as they were and wanted no substantial changes. Because public opinion had not been adequately prepared, O'Neill was regarded as a disturber of the peace by many Protestants and a foot-dragger by many Catholics who wanted a faster rate of progress.

Both the civil rights movement and the Protestant backlash began almost simultaneously in 1966-68. When a Catholic family in Dungannon was denied housing and an unmarried Protestant secretary given the house instead, the modern Ulster civil rights movement can be said to have been born. Demonstrations and petitions began. Cases of discrimination were publicized. For example, in the 53 percent Catholic county of Fermanagh, only 32 of 370 local government jobs (9 percent) were held by Catholics. Trouble began when civil rights marches were banned by Home Affairs Minister William Craig, and then attacked by police and Protestant militants.

The next phase, 1969-71, was characterized by the radicalization of the civil rights movement, Protestant desire to reassert traditional law and order, the resignation of Prime Minister O'Neill and the sending of British troops to Ulster in the summer of 1969 to prevent the possible Protestant massacre of Catholics. (One pro-IRA priest I interviewed claimed that the troops were really sent to prop up the Stormont government, not to aid the Catholics.) Catholics welcomed the soldiers initially, but terrorist activities by the IRA added a new and volatile element to an already explosive situation. In April 1969, fiery civil rights advocate Miss Bernadette Devlin was elected as an independent "Unity" candidate to the British parliament from the Mid-Ulster constituency.

The situation moved from bad to worse as the next Prime Minister, Mr. Chichester-Clark resigned and was replaced by Mr. Faulkner. The Royal Ulster Constabulary had been disarmed and the special constabulary abolished. Attitudes in both communities were hardening, and compromise rendered more unlikely. As terrorism escalated, the Stormont government, with the tacit approval of the new Conservative government in Britain, introduced internment of suspected terrorists in August 1971. The Catholic community was outraged and the nation veered toward open civil war.

It soon became evident that the Stormont government was unable to govern effectively. The long rumored "direct rule" was imposed by London in late March, 1972. Stormont was suspended for one year and a new administrative official, Mr. William Whitelaw, was named by London to oversee the province. This was surely one of the toughest assignments ever given a government official at any time in British or Irish history. It is generally conceded that Mr. Whitelaw has done a creditable job.

During the last year, the British government has tried to reassure both communities and work steadily for the reduction of violence and the eventual return of some modified local control. The border referendum, indicating a majority of Ulstermen want to remain in the United Kingdom, and a White Paper setting forth plans for a new Regional Assembly for Ulster have been accomplished. Local government elections in May and the Assembly elections in June 1973, bring us to the uncertain but hopeful present.

An Ulster Chronology

1600   Plantation of Ulster by Scotch-Irish Protestants

1641   Massacre of Protestants

1649   Retaliatory massacre of Catholics by Cromwell

1690   Battle of the Boyne—Protestant Ascendancy in Kingdom guaranteed

1795   Foundation of Orange Order to defend Protestant religion and the liberties of England

1798   United Irish Societies established—Temporary Presbyterian-Roman Catholic unity

1830   Beginning of anti-Catholic agitation

1857   Drew Sermon results in communal rioting

1859   Evangelical Revival sweeps province

1886   Sectarian violence—Lord Randolph Churchill warns against Home Rule—"Ulster will fight and Ulster will be right."

1912   Solemn League and Covenant against Home Rule— Ulster Volunteer Force founded

1921   Foundation of State of Northern Ireland and incorporation into the United Kingdom.

1922   Special Powers Act promulgated

1935   Foundation of Ulster Protestant Action to defend

Protestants in employment opportunities; violent riots rock Belfast.

1937   Lord Craigavon declares "a Protestant Parliament for a Protestant people."

1938   *Ulster Protestant* founded (militant anti-Catholic monthly)

1940-45 WW-II—Ulster Protestants volunteer in large numbers to fight Nazism. Irish Free State neutral. Lord Brookeborough urges Protestant employers to hire only loyal Protestants.

1949   Ireland Act declares:
        (1) The border could not be changed without the consent of Stormont;
        (2) The UK would not intervene in Northern Ireland internal affairs except to control a breakdown of law and order.

1954-58 The IRA starts raids in Ulster—187 people are interned in Ulster and 206 in Eire.

1963   Captain O'Neill becomes Premier of Northern Ireland.

1965   Captain O'Neill invites Sean Lemass, Prime Minister of Eire, to go to Belfast to discuss matters of common interest. The question of the border was not on the agenda.

1966   The Rev. Ian Paisley organizes demonstrations against "Romeward" trend in the Presbyterian Church. Convicted of unlawful assembly and later imprisoned.
        Captain O'Neill proscribes extremist Ulster Volunteer Force.
        Catholics celebrate 50th Anniversary of Easter Rising of 1916.
        Orange Resolution against ecumenism
        Protestant Telegraph founded to enunciate Paisleyite views.

35

1967	Formation of Northern Ireland Civil Rights Movement
1968	Civil Rights March in Londonderry, October, although banned by Mr. Craig, Minister of Home Affairs. The Royal Ulster Constabulary (RUC) reacts roughly and there are more demonstrations in Belfast.
	In November the Londonderry Commission is set up to deal with economic grievances. An Ombudsman is appointed to investigate grievances. Mr. Paisley leads a march against the reforms. Mr. Craig is dismissed and Captain O'Neill embarks on a program of reforms dealing with housing and local government.
1969	A Civil Rights march from Belfast to Londonderry is permitted in January. There is a clash at Burntollet between the marchers and Protestant extremists. The RUC enters the Bogside where a later Commission of Enquiry alleges that assaults and misconduct occurred.
April	Captain O'Neill resigns and is replaced by Major Chichester-Clark. Miss Bernadette Devlin secures a seat at Westminster, winning the Mid-Ulster by election.
August	Protestant-Catholic violence erupts. British troops sent in to keep the peace, sharing responsibility for security with Stormont.
	The Cameron Commission is set up to investigate the disorders.
October	The B Specials are disbanded. Measures are taken to recruit a new force, known as the Ulster Defence Regiment.
Nov.	RUC disarmed.
	Evangelical Protestant Society expands efforts to convert Roman Catholics to Protestant Faith

1970

Jan.   Firearms Act and Prevention of Incitement to Hatred Act are passed but not enforced.

April   The Rev. Ian Paisley is elected to Stormont from Bannside.

June   Minimum Sentences Act enjoins mandatory sentences for rioters. Mr. Frank McManus, Civil Rights leader, elected to Westminster.

        Paisley elected to Westminster from North Antrim.

August A ban on all parades and marches for six months is imposed by Stormont.

Dec.   Stormont introduces major reforms for local government.

1971

Feb.   The government refuses to round up licensed guns despite the ire of opposition MPs who fear that some of the clubs were fronts for illegal, para-military organizations. (20% of adult males own guns in Ulster.)

March   Over 6,000 shipyard workers, Protestant and Catholic, march through the streets of Belfast to demand the internment of the IRA.

        Major Chichester-Clark resigns and is replaced by Mr. Faulkner.

May   The newly founded Ulster Deference Regiment recruits at this time and is expected to have about 5,000 men by the end of the year. Its main task is to guard vulnerable points and roadblocks.

June   Cardinal Conway indicates integrated education might be acceptable.

July   The Social Democratic and Labour Party withdraws from Stormont over the shooting of civilians in Londonderry.

August Internment is introduced.

37

Many refugees fled to Eire, the Irish government setting up camps for them. (Most later returned.)

Mr. Lynch supports the campaign of civil disobedience. This campaign included the nonpayment of rates and rents which angered the Protestants.

Sept.
Cardinal Conway finally condemns the violence. An estimated 8,000 people fled from the center of Belfast in the last six weeks. The lines between the Protestant and Catholic working classes are now rigidly drawn.

A jury fails to bring in a verdict in Belfast in the first prosecution under the Prevention of Incitement to Hatred Act.

Oct.
Tripartite talks with Mr. Lynch, Mr. Faulkner, and Mr. Heath

Senator Kennedy attacks the British government for its Ulster policy.

A leading Belfast Catholic, Dr. Gerard Newe, was given a Cabinet post to try to make contact with various elements in the Catholic community.

Nov.
Mr. Craig starts a new group called Ulster Vanguard meant to preserve a strict Loyalist line.

Ireland threatens to take the case of the internees to the International Court of Justice.

A senatorial resolution co-sponsored by Senator Edward Kennedy, calls for the withdrawal of British troops.

Mr. Paisley forms a new party, the Democratic Unionists.

Dec.
An Ulster Protestant senator is assassinated.

A new group in the U.S.A. called the American Committee for Ulster Justice is established.

The IRA Provisionals present a program—
    (a) The end of violence by the British Army
    (b) The abolition of Stormont

(c) A free election to establish a regional Parliament

(d) The release of all political prisoners

(e) Compensation for all who had suffered British violence.

1972

January   The banned civil rights march in Londonderry takes place and 13 people are killed.

There is enormous indignation in the Republic, and the event attracts world interest.

Feb.   Miss Bernadette Devlin physically attacks the British Home Secretary, Mr. Maulding, in the House.

The British Embassy in Dublin is burned to the ground.

Dr. Hillery, Ireland's Foreign Minister, calls on the U.S. and other countries friendly to Britain to persuade the British government to change its policy towards Ulster.

Mr. Lynch condemns the burning of the British Embassy.

The Alliance Party founded to reconcile Protestants and Catholics.

March   Pastor Jack Glass, a Glasgow militant Protestant leader, threatens that a Protestant army of 5,000 could be raised in Glasgow to fight in Northern Ireland, if the government attempts to alter the constitution of the Province.

Mr. Heath announces that direct rule would be imposed on Ulster by Easter. Mr. William Whitelaw will become Secretary of State for the Province. The main points of the political initiative are: (1) the transfer of responsibility for law and order in the province to Westminster; (2) the suspension for at least one year of the powers of the Stormont parliament and government; (3) periodic plebiscites in Ulster on whether there should be a change in the

39

border with Eire; (4) a start on phasing out internment.

Mr. William Craig, leader of the Ulster Vanguard Movement, calls on Protestant workers to shut down the province.

A strike of almost the whole Protestant working force brings business and industrial life to a virtual halt. Huge crowds, unequivocally rejecting direct rule, attend rallies throughout the six counties.

April   Thousands of Roman Catholics attend ceremonies commemorating the Easter uprising of 1916.

A meeting of the Women Together Movement, which seeks peace in the Province, was broken up by members of the Provisional IRA.

Random sectarian assassinations continue—121 by December (81 Roman Catholic, 40 Protestants). Atrocities such as church burnings and machine gun attacks on funerals horrify nation. Massive bombings continue. Much of Belfast lies in ruins. Applications for emigration to New Zealand, Canada, Australia increase.

Dec.   Referendum to remove "special position" of Roman Catholic Church in the Republic passes by 85 percent. Considered meaningless by Ulster Protestants.

1973
March   The Border Referendum is boycotted by Catholics. Protestants vote 99 percent in favor of maintaining British connection.

May   Local government elections

June   Regional Assembly elections

October   Protestant and Catholic churchmen meet in Dundalk, County Louth, Ireland.

3.   Is It A Religious War?

"If there were less bigoted religion in Ulster
and more Christianity, there would be far less
problems."
                              Bernadette Devlin

When one considers the question of church-state relations
in Northern Ireland, it is instructive to look first at the question of religious liberty. As part of the United Kingdom, there is
a high degree of free exercise permitted to all religions. Both
Protestants and Roman Catholics may worship freely, establish
church buildings and auxiliary enterprises, advertise in the
press and media, make converts, publish religious periodicals,
establish seminaries for clerical training, own property, and
propagate their religious opinions. Civil divorce is permitted, as
is the distribution and sale of contraceptives for family
planning. No laws restrict adoptions by couples of mixed
marriages. No church may censor literature, the cinema, or the
theatre. The government does not interfere in the internal
working of the churches or the selection of ecclesiastical
officials. The contrast with many other nations is obvious.

There are a number of areas where religion undoubtedly
influences political events and issues. Britain's liberalized
abortion law of 1967 was not applied to Northern Ireland,

41

probably because of the innate conservatism of both Protestants and Roman Catholics. Protestant clergy have been prominent in enforcing Sunday closing statutes in parts of Ulster. Though there is no religious test for public office, Roman Catholics have been under-represented in the Stormont parliament, primarily through gerrymandering.

Let us consider the complex question of whether the present conflict can truly be considered a religious war. Americans, I think, frequently ask this question above all others. Since the intensity of the violence surrounding the 1968-69 civil rights movement began to attract world attention, the two warring participants have been designated as Catholics and Protestants. News accounts frequently mentioned the Catholic-Protestant clashes and intimidations of neighbors because of religious affiliation. Mobs which attacked and burned Catholic homes were labeled "Protestant" while mobs which assaulted British soldiers were labeled "Catholic." During the conflict, distinctly sectarian slogans have been used and sectarian rationales have been propounded. Some church property has been destroyed, though it was relatively late in the period of violent eruptions that churches, church schools or church-affiliated lodges were damaged or destroyed.

Two Roman Catholic churches were burned in early 1973. St. Anthony's in East Belfast was especially hard hit when a mob of 2,000 Protestant youths desecrated the church's altar and sculpture, smashing everything in their sight and terrorizing the priests. On the other hand, Rev. Martin Smyth, a Presbyterian minister and chaplain of the Grand Orange Lodge of Ireland, charges in *The Battle for Northern Ireland* that many Protestant churches have been destroyed since 1969. They are:

1. Jonesborough Presbyterian Church Co. Down, burnt in July 1969;
2. Donegall Road Methodist Church, Belfast, burnt in August 1969;
3. Luther, Church of Ireland, Whiterock, vandalized and

deconsecrated in 1970 after one hundred years of witness;
4. Springfield Road Presbyterian, Belfast—a virile new church with a thriving Sunday School closed in 1970. In spite of the community leadership by its minister, Rev. Cecil Courtney, its parish was steadily taken over by Republicans and the large Protestant community, inadequately protected, had to flee to other parts;
5. Salvation Army Goodwill Centre, off Roden Street, Belfast, closed and members ordered out by IRA gunmen in summer 1971;
6. Aldersgate Methodist Youth Centre, Belfast, damaged by bomb, 1971;
7. Cliftonpark and Antrim Road Baptist Churches, Belfast, damaged by bomb blast in 1971;
8. Dublin Road, Belfast, Salvation Army Citadel destroyed and a member killed as result of burning of adjoining warehouse in December 1971;
9. Dromore (Co. Tyrone) Parish Hall destroyed in January 1972;
10. Spamount Congregational Church, Belfast, severely vandalized.

A number of Roman Catholic schools have also been firebombed.

The *Belfast Telegraph* reported in the Autumn of 1973 that since the trouble began in 1968, 68 Protestant churches have been damaged and 5 destroyed, while 45 Catholic churches have been damaged and 3 destroyed.

So, it appears to outsiders to be a genuine religious war, a tragic flashback to the 16th or 17th century. But is it?

This is one of the most difficult questions I attempted to tackle in this investigation. In the beginning I was generally convinced that, in a sense, this was a religious war. Let me explain first by defining what it is not. It is not a theological war, everyone would agree here. No one is bombing or shooting in the name of "justification by faith" or "the Immaculate Conception." By no means are people fighting over intricate points of doctrine. Neither are they fighting to obliterate the other religion as such. Only the most discredited wild-eyed extremists, such as Johnny McKeague's Red Hand outfit, really talks about exterminating the opposition. But it seemed to me, and still does partially, that the religious dimension to the struggle was very significant.

It is pretty clearly evident that Protestants and Catholics are struggling for cultural and political dominance of their society. Some very distinctive attributes, especially on the Protestant side, of the political and economic struggles are religious in origin, as we shall see.

Though the top church leaders have recently decried interpretations of a religious war, the leadership of both religions has a stake in the outcome of this conflict.

The strange irony that I encountered in many interviews is that the clergymen were the most likely to deny that this dispute is in any way a religious one! Perhaps they are ashamed of the manifold lack of essential Christian virtues shown by their coreligionists. Perhaps they realized how heavy the burden of past hatreds hangs over the present. The Presbyterian Church, in an official resolution deploring the interfaith antagonisms, denied that clergy had any special political knowledge or any real ability to control the outcome of the conflict. The clergy seem to deny any complicity in creating the interfaith hostilities.

Canon Hamilton of Washington National Cathedral, a native of Belfast, urged me to reconsider my thesis that this was in any significant way a religious war. It is a political and economic struggle between communities who happen to be Protestant and Catholic, he said. It is essentially a modern version of the age-old struggle between colonialists and the colonized. The roots of the conflict began before the Reformation, and the British colonization policies have more to do with the present conflict than religion, he felt. He believed that Protestants would have no real objections to a united Ireland if they could be assured that their standard of living would not decline. He felt that Protestant objections to a society where Roman Catholic social and moral teachings heavily influence civil legislation were relatively minor and could be modified if the economic situation of the Republic improved.

Father Sean McManus, an Ulster native and brother of politician Frank McManus, and now assigned to the archdiocese of Baltimore, categorically denied the religious implications of the conflict. There have been no martyrs to Jesus Christ, only to Ireland, he stated. He noted his dismay that Americans believe that Irish Christians are butchering each other in Jesus' name. This is British government propaganda, he asserted. "The British have used the religious fears of Protestants to maintain their ascendancy in the North of Ireland. They have used religious differences to drive a wedge between Irish people for political reasons." Whenever there were distinct possibilities that Protestant and Catholic Irishmen might be willing to bury their differences and work for a United Ireland, as in 1791-98, the British waved the "No Popery" flag. McManus denied that Catholics hate Protestants or Protestanism, though acknowledging that much Protestant sentiment toward Catholicism is hostile. He denied that Protestants would massacre Catholics in a pogrom, if British troops withdrew. (This was one of the main reasons the British government and Mr. Whitelaw have given for their refusal to leave Ulster.) Like Canon Hamilton, Father McManus emphasized the nonreligious aspects of the war.

Irish diplomat and scholar Conor Cruise O'Brien tried to resolve this difficult dilemma, replying "Is it a religious quarrel? I believe the answer is yes, but with significant qualifications . . . . It is inescapably a conflict between groups defined by religion." O'Brien accused the churches of "encouraging, exalting and extending the kind of tribal-sectarian self-righteousness which forms a culture in which violence so easily multiplies."

Avro Manhattan, characteristically, blames the Roman Catholic hierarchy for most of the trouble, claiming that they

45

want to destroy the last stronghold of militant Protestantism and Catholicize all of Ireland. This is the unchanging Roman Catholic strategy for world conquest in Mr. Manhattan's view.

My own belief is that, though serious economic and political factors sustain the civil conflict, the religious element is dominant. This is a struggle of two communities holding fervent religious views. If it were not for religiously based antagonism and misunderstanding, the economic and political questions could eventually be solved. If both religious communities could be assured that their liberty will be preserved in the future, much of the irrationality of the present Ulster conflict would be removed. When religion enters an already existing conflict and shapes that conflict in an emotional direction, terrible events often occur. That is the lesson history teaches.

How deeply involved have the churches been in Ulster's recent crisis? Have they helped to stimulate the violence or have they been a force for peace? This is another of the complex, difficult to answer questions that arises when one thinks of Ulster. Of course, it is fair to say that neither the churches nor the clergy have actively participated in the violence and terror nor have they encouraged it in any way. The real question is whether they did enough to prevent it.

The public pronouncements of both Protestant and Roman Catholic churchmen have been quite commendable. All deplore violence and destruction, though, as we shall soon see, Cardinal Conway rather qualified his condemnation and blamed the Protestants explicitly for their part in the 1969 riots. The clergy have helped to calm mobs during volatile demonstrations. But two points need to be made, which will help to unravel this mystery. As I shall demonstrate in much of this book, the churches have created an atmosphere of suspicion and intolerance because of the way they treat the other religion in their writings, sermons, etc. All too often they have helped to mold an atmosphere where hatred and fanaticism are normal and acceptable. On the other hand, it is safe to say that in no

46

society, however formally religious, do all people adhere to the positive guidelines that all churches seek to create in individual relations. The churches, even if they preach tolerance and brotherhood, are unable to control the actions of all their members, especially in times of trial and stress. This is true in all societies. Let us look at how some of the churches have responded to events since 1969. In the summer of 1969, events in Belfast and Londonderry pushed Ulster to the brink of open sectarian war. Catholics charged that armed Protestant mobs invaded their neighborhoods in Belfast. This is how three leading churchmen reacted.

Cardinal Conway, speaking on behalf of five Roman Catholic bishops in Ulster:

". . . We deeply regret that the true picture of these events has been greatly obscured by official statements and by the character of the coverage given in certain influential news media.

"The fact is that on Thursday and Friday of last week the Catholic district of Falls and Ardoyne were invaded by mobs equipped with machine-guns and other firearms. A community which was virtually defenceless was swept by gunfire and streets of Catholic homes were systematically set on fire. We entirely reject the hypothesis that the origin of last week's tragedy was an armed insurrection.

". . . In this contest we regret that the full evidence available regarding the action of some members of the police in the early hours of the morning in the Bogside area of Derry last January has never been made public. We are convinced that in the terror evoked in the people of Bogside on that night lies the basic explanation of recent events in Derry.

"In this period of crisis we call upon all our people to remain calm and to avoid all words or actions which could in any way increase tension. We ask them not to allow bitterness or hatred to enter into their hearts, to remember that Protestants in general are good Christian people and to commence the re-building of community relations with Christian faith and hope."

Rev. Donald Gillies, a leading Presbyterian pastor, said:

47

"On behalf of a number of Protestant ministers who laboured day and night in the troubled Ardoyne area I must make the strongest objection to the latest attempt by Cardinal Conway and five bishops to place the blame for recent troubles on one side only.

"This is a complete fabrication and the type of thing we expect and get from certain politicians. This is not the way to restore confidence, to remove suspicion and rebuild community relations. Unlike the Cardinal and bishops we were eye-witnesses to the tragic events of the past few weeks in the Hooker Street-Disraeli Street district and we must say that the bombs and shots from what Cardinal Conway describes as a "virtually defenceless area" were responsible for the outbreak of hostility and for appropriate action by the police and retaliatory action by Protestants.

"We deplore as much as anyone the violence and destruction by some Protestants but in all fairness it was time that the same publicity should be given to the aggression and provocation which helped to bring this about."

The Moderator of the Presbyterian Church, Dr. John Carson, stated:

"The Cardinal's statement will, in my view, be regarded by many as not likely to add to the spirit of mutual trust and confidence on which we must try to build. It will, I fear, confirm the fears and suspicions of Protestant people and exacerbate the tension which prevails throughout the province. It has been freely admitted by reasonable people that provocations and excesses were committed by both sides. A thorough investigation, and history, will give the final judgment on these and we can reasonably leave it like that. The truth must prevail."

A more militant view was expressed by the *Bulwark*, published by the Evangelical Protestant Society:

". . . As long as Popery reigns and rules in Eire, and has so many devotees in Ulster, there cannot be lasting peace. Irish Romanism breeds disloyalty to the British Throne and hatred to the Government of Northern Ireland so how can there be peace?"

Here one can see how difficult it was, even for prominent men of God, to respond in other than traditional sectarian terms.

Similar statements were made when other crises occurred.

When internment was introduced in 1971 Cardinal Conway denounced it as "a terrible power to give to any political authority." Though Conway undoubtedly reflected Catholic anger at conditions in Ulster, he finally denounced all violence (on August 11, 1971,) He said:

". . . I fully understand the deep emotion and frustration and to some extent the foreboding which exists among the Catholic population as a whole at the present time.

"But, I think that at a time like this one ought to be careful not to let emotion, however natural and however strong, lead one into situations or courses of action which are in fact foolish and which can very often result in serious injury or death."

Despite this statement, Rev. John Thompson of the Belfast Presbyterian Synod was still not satisfied:

"We, on our part, as Protestants and Presbyterians, may feel that it is very hard to cooperate with those, many of whom seem directly or indirectly to condone violence and whose utterances in the past have been equivocal."

Some religious leaders exhibited greater humility and perception. The Church of Ireland *Gazette* commented on August 22, 1971:

"No Christian worthy of the name can possibly hear without shame the words 'Protestant' and 'Catholic' used to describe mobs bent on death and destruction . . .

Dr. Eric Gallagher, a Methodist clergyman and Superintendent of the Belfast Central Mission, says that "Tragically, the contribution of the churches has been to date, however, well-intentioned, too little, too late, and too ineffective." Gallagher has warned churchmen to face up to the problem of violence and desensitivity to human suffering. He charged that none of the churches has frankly faced the problem of violence.

49

In his booklet "A Better Way for Irish Protestants and Roman Catholics," Rev. Gallagher called for:

". . . imaginative official action by the Churches, symbolic acts of love, courage, respect and love by significant people in the Churches, and—above all—new dimensions in the thinking and actions of ordinary people."

Gallagher added:

"It is a plain fact that in spite of all the welcome signs and developments of recent years, there is a very considerable religious content in the bitterness and suspicion which bedevil so much of Northern Ireland life particularly."

Rev. Jack Weir, the general secretary of the Presbyterian Church in Ireland, emphasized that Protestant and Catholic leaders "have met 20 or 30 times since 1969, but it seems that churches are not too effective in political disputes." He urged Catholics to slow down their demands a bit and let the Protestants adjust to the political and economic changes in Ulster. He believes that most Protestants have reconciled themselves to change and have already made considerable concessions.

May 23, 1973 a letter signed by the top leadership of the Roman Catholic, Methodist, Presbyterian and Anglican churches in Ireland again reiterated their curious belief that:

"The conflict is not primarily religious in character. It is based rather on political and social issues with deep historical roots. Undoubtedly, again for reasons that are largely historical, the political, and social divisions have religious overtones. But this is far from saying that the conflict between extremists here is anything even remotely resembling a religious war."

The Roman Catholic bishops of the Irish Republic and Northern Ireland denounced "all campaigns of violence" in a Lenten statement issued on March 30, 1973. The statement said, in part:

"The continuing violence in (Northern Ireland) with its callous disregard for the sacredness of human life has shocked the Christian conscience of the world.

". . . In God's name, we call upon all who are seeking political ends by violent means to defer to the manifest will of the people of all Ireland and bring all campaigns of violence to an end."

Despite the recent, perhaps belated, attempts of the churches to do something positive and constructive about inter-faith tensions, the Rev. Donald Gillies warned in June 1973 that "the greatest tragedy in Northern Ireland today is the hardening of hearts, the suppression of love, the growth of fear, and the rise of hatred."

While dealing with the churches, it is important to inquire into the Vatican's involvement, if any, in the conflict. The Vatican officially remained silent until the summer of 1971, though the Pope had briefly expressed sorrow about the 1969 events. *L'Osservatore Romano,* the Vatican daily newspaper, declared that the root cause of the trouble was the "absurd discriminations against the Catholic population, which have given rise to conditions of economic, civic and social inferiority." Vatican press officer Federico Alessandrini con-demned the introduction of internment in the Vatican Sunday newspaper *L'Osservatore Della Dominica* as reminiscent of the French Revolution.

At a general Sunday audience in Castel Gandolfo, the Pope's summer residence, Pope Paul blamed "the adoption of exceptional security measures which are strongly resented by a part of the population." Though calling for peace, the Pope implied that there would never be peace in Ulster until Catholics were treated with justice. Such a statement was interpreted by many Catholics to be a green light for continuation of Catholic opposition to the Ulster government. The Pope's statement, however, did not set well with a leading English Catholic Conservative member of Parliament. Mr. John Biggs-Davison, a supporter of Ulster unionism, sent a letter to the pontiff saying, in part:

"As a loyal supporter of the Pope's authority and

51

teaching, who defended in public the papal encyclical on birth control, I ask the Holy See to reflect upon the dismay of Her Majesty's loyal Catholic subjects and of all British people of goodwill, if Rome condemns measures taken in good faith to defend the United Kingdom and its people against murder and terrorism."

Nothing more about Ulster was said officially at the Vatican until the spring of 1973 when two eye-popping events occurred. After meeting with Prime Minister Heath, the Vatican endorsed the White Paper as a good solution to the conflict. Then, the Provisional wing of the IRA in Belfast denounced the Pope mildly as "misinformed" about the situation in Ulster. Imagine the IRA criticizing the Pope!

Then, in a shocking statement, Vatican press officer Alessandrini implied that demands for full reunion of Ireland would be unjust to Protestants because Protestants would become a minority subject to oppression. "To substitute for an oppressive domination another analogous domination is certainly not being just," Alessandrini noted. The Irish Embassy in London reacted sharply. "There is no oppression of the minority community in southern Ireland," said an embassy spokesman angrily. Alessandrini had also condemned the IRA.

The most recent public utterance was Pope Paul's encouragement of prayers for peace in Northern Ireland as a preparation for the 1975 Holy Year.

And, finally, an editorial by Ian Paisley from *The Protestant Telegraph* of June 9, 1973.

The usual bunch of ecumenists, declaring themselves as voicing the unanimous opinion of their respective members, have informed the Pope that they have the sole explanation to the "Irish" troubles. "Cardinal" Conway, Dr. Simms, Rev. Lindsay and Rev. Lynas as leaders of the four main churches have written to "Cardinal" John Willebrands, president of the Vatican secretariat to unite the Churches under Roman rule and to Dr. Phillip Potter, general secretary of the W.C.C. They state that the troubles are based on political and social issues with deep historical roots and they deplore the fact that the situation has been described as religious in character.

Such an analysis we have come to expect from the Communists; that is, the trouble is of economic and social origin. Now the Ancient Order of Ecumenists has joined in with the cry—"it is not religion!"

The fact is the troubles stem from the interference of Popes and Popery in Irish affairs. Pope Urban inspired Henry II to invade, subjugate and control Ireland, and during the past eight hundred years that aim has been encouraged by successive Popes. Rebellion, war and subversion have been openly commended by the Popes. Pope Paul should have been accused of the crimes which the I.R.A. have committed in the name of Popery. He is the guilty one, and those that associate with him in the religio-political plot to destroy Ulster must share the blame and the punishment.

This is a religious war—a battle between Truth and Error, Light and Darkness, Bible Protestantism and Popery.

It is sad, but necessary, to judge the churches and their leaders rather harshly because of their failure to communicate a Christian spirit of understanding and justice to their flock. As the Church of Ireland *Gazette* remarked in 1971:

If they (the clergy) had tried and failed, if they had come together in an effort to find a solution, if they had shown themselves willing to explore a way that might lead not to a "Protestant" or Catholic" victory, but to Christian peace and justice, their shame might not now lie so heavy. (Quoted by Howard G. Hageman, "The Irish Question," *The Church Herald,* Nov. 26, 1971)

The Voice of Ulster

'Tis the voice of Ulster calling from across the narrow sea ;
Of Ulster waiting, watching, before the dark To Be.
'Tis the voice of Ulster calling, in the crisis of her fate :
Will ye hear it, oh, my brothers, will ye hearken, ere too late ?

'Tis the voice of Ulster calling : it is borne upon the blast,
From the high-built walls of Derry, from the harbours of
    Belfast ;
From the cornfields and the flaxfields, from the hills and
    shores and bays.
'Tis the voice of Ulster calling, at the parting of the ways.

'Tis the voice of Ulster calling ; and her noble heart may bleed
As she pictures all her labours made the prey of guile and
    greed,
And the clink of shipwright's hammer and the whirring of the
    loom
Hushed for ever in the silence and the darkness of the tomb.

'Tis the voice of Ulster calling, and the hand of Ulster too
Holds on high the flag of England, bids it flutter to the blue.
Will you tear it from her fingers, will you drag the banner
    down,
And unfold instead the emblem of the Harp without the
    Crown ?

'Tis the voice of Ulster calling : but her heart is bold and high,
And ere she forfeit freedom 'she will know the reason why'.
And, if her friends forsake her, and faith be false and fled,
Then the 'Bloody Hand' of Ulster may be dyed a deeper red.

'Tis the voice of Ulster calling : shall her cry be all in vain ?
Shall the Union bonds be broken and the One be henceforth
    Twain ?
'Tis the voice of Ulster calling, in the crisis of her fate :
Ye will hear it, oh, my brothers, ye will hearken ere too late.

We are grateful to a correspondent who sent the above poem to us.
It was originally published at an earlier time of crisis.

4.   Ian Paisley and the Orange Order

Two of the mainstays of the Protestant ascendancy today are the Orange Order and the movement led by the Reverend Ian Paisley.

"I have hated the enemies of God with a perfect hate."

The acknowledged leader of the Protestant militants is a tall, articulate demagogue, the Rev. Ian R.K. Paisley, moderator of the Free Presbyterian Church of Ulster. Part buffoon, part messiah, Paisley assumed the leadership of the "No Popery and No Surrender" Protestant elements in 1966. Though most Ameircan and British journalists regarded Paisley as a bizarre figure out of the 17th century, his political adeptness and sagacity have been overlooked. He is, in fact, the sharpest political operator in Northern Ireland. The depth of Paisley's support was exemplified by a fiery-eyed, little, gray-haired lady who told this author, "He is the Man of God for our time."

Paisley was born in Ballymena, in heavily Protestant County Antrim in 1927 and attended Ballymena Technical College. At age 16 Paisley enrolled in the Barrie School of Evangelism in Wales but switched a year later to the Theological Hall of the Reformed Presbyterian Church in Belfast from which he received his preaching license at age 19. After his ordination in 1945 he established the Ravenhill

Evangelistic Mission in the tough shipyard district of East Belfast, and eventually established the Free Presbyterian Church in 1951 when he became horrified at the alleged liberalism of the established Presbyterian Church. He then founded the National Union of Protestants and was appointed a chaplain to the Junior Orangemen after his ordination. From 1951 to 1968 his little sect grew from 1,000 to about 15,000 adherents in 12 churches scattered around Ulster. He even opened a branch in the Irish Republic in 1972.

In the late '50s Paisley disrupted a meeting addressed by prominent Methodist ecumenist Dr. Donald Soper (Lord Soper), and was fined for causing a breach of the peace. In 1964 Paisley fielded four unsuccessful "Protestant Unionist" candidates for the Belfast corporation (the local government). Along the way he acquired some degrees from American diploma-mills—Pioneer Theological Seminary, Rockford, Illinois and Burton College in Colorado.

A magnetic orator and a fervent believer that his cause is the cause of God, Paisley surfaced as a political agitator during the so-called "Tricolour Riots" of September and October, 1964. Paisley was incensed that some Catholic Republicans had dared to fly the Tricolour flag of Eire during the general election campaign then underway. He led his militant supporters into the Catholic area and removed the offending symbol of treason. Sectarian violence erupted again, for the first time since the frightful occurrences in 1935. Paisley filled the Ulster Hall every Sunday night as thousands came to revel in his harangues.

By 1966 Paisley was convinced that Protestant Ulster was in danger of betrayal by the moderate Protestant leadership and the progressive O'Neill regime. In the summer of 1966 Paisley led sympathizers into Cromac Square, a Catholic neighborhood where no Protestant processions had been allowed since 1935. Not unexpectedly violence occurred. Paisley then organized a violent demonstration against the "Romeward" trend of the Presbyterian Church. Paisley

56

denounced the World Council of Churches and tried to disrupt the Presbyterian Assembly. His supporters terrified the wife of Ulster's Governor General. Paisley established a virulent fortnightly for the exposition of true Protestantism called *The Protestant Telegraph.* The paper promised to proclaim fearlessly Protestant truth against Romish error. The paper now reaches over 25,000 subscribers.

For refusing to pay a fine for his part in fomenting these riots, Paisley was sentenced to three months in jail for unlawful assembly, where he wrote a commentary on the Epistle to the Romans and exhorted his followers to remain firm. On the day of his release, his supporters carried him away in a car adorned with a banner, "Behold the Lamb of God."

Paisley spent the next three years strengthening the Protestant cause in Ulster, establishing contacts with Dr. Carl McIntyre's Twentieth Century Reformation Movement in Collingswood, New Jersey and invading ecumenical gatherings in the established churches. McIntyre gave Paisley a boost in his *Christian Beacon* and sponsored Paisley's speaking engagements in the United States. Paisley often appears at McIntyre's Christian Admiral Hotel Conference on the Jersey Shore. Paisley also visits Bob Jones University in Greenville, South Carolina, where he got his honorary "doctorate." Dr. Bob Jones dedicated Paisley's impressive new church on the Ravenhill Road in East Belfast in October 1969. The new building, seating 3,000 and built at a cost in excess of £150,000 ($360,000) is Paisley's new sounding board to excoriate the dreaded enemy.

Paisley's forays have an almost comic-opera quality about them. He and his supporters, brandishing huge Bibles and singing martial hymns, such as "Our Fathers Knew Thee Rome of Old and Evil Is Thy Fame," disrupted ecumenical services at St. Paul's Cathedral in London, Canterbury Cathedral, the Anglican Church in Rome, and the general assembly of the Church of Scotland. Paisley, to top it all off, read Revelation 18 in front of St. Peter's in Rome, until the police carted him off!

Paisley's *bête noire* is the Archbishop of Canterbury, who has been pursuing an ecumenical entente with Rome for a decade. Paisley regards him as a Romanist in disguise and a betrayer of Protestant England. Paisley tried to disrupt the Pope's visit to Geneva, Switzerland and Australia, but the governmental authorities refused him a visa.

His bizarre adventures have invariably been disruptive. He threatened a massive demonstration of 100,000 to protest Anglican Bishop Moorman's proposed address at St. Anne's Anglican Cathedral in Belfast in February 1967. Bishop Moorman, an Anglo-Catholic ecumenist, was personally invited by the Dean of St. Anne's. Fear of hostility, insult or violence caused the cancellation of the Bishop's appearance. Another capitulation to extremism had occurred.

In February 1969 Paisley challenged Prime Minister O'Neill in the Prime Minister's home constituency, Bannside. Though given no chance of victory by most observers, Paisley shocked the daylights out of O'Neill and the moderate Protestant community by polling 39 percent of the vote to the Prime Minister's 47 percent (a Catholic "Peoples Democracy" candidate trailed with 14 percent). Paisley had polled 45 percent of the Protestant vote in a constituency where he was relatively unknown and where O'Neill had not been challenged in 24 years! This indicated the depth of Protestant belligerence and feelings of betrayal by the establishment. Political observers should have taken notice of Paisley instead of regarding him as a clown, as his strength continued to grow.

In April 1970 Captain O'Neill was named by the Queen to the House of Lords (though he had resigned from the Prime Ministership in disgust a year before). This necessitated a by-election, which Paisley promptly entered. This time, sentiments having been hardened by the escalating violence, Mr. Paisley secured 54 percent of the Protestant vote and carried the constituency. Militant diehard Protestant Ulster now had a voice in Stormont. Interestingly, Mr. Paisley told the cheering crowds on the night of his victory that "you won't have to be

58

oppressed by the landed gentry anymore." This populist orientation of the Paisleyite movement is generally unappreciated by many observers, but is a real factor in the support for Mr. Paisley among the Protestant working class and farm community.

Paisley parried his new-found success into another smashing victory in the June 1970 Parliamentary election for Westminster. Paisley convinced his aggrieved listeners that he could be 'their' voice in London—the voice of Protestant truth. He entered the North Antrim constituency, the heaviest Protestant stronghold in Ulster. The moderate Protestant establishment and Unionists were visibly frightened, but confident that Paisley, running as a Protestant Unionist, couldn't possibly defeat an entrenched member of Parliament. They underestimated the depth of sentiment for one who spoke the traditional language, stood staunchly for established truths and promised never to surrender to the enemies of Ulster. Paisley won 24,156 to 21,430. Paisley's victory sent a shockwave to the Roman Catholic community and to moderates and liberals throughout the United Kingdom.

Paisley lost no time in defending the ultra-Protestant position in the Mother of Parliaments. His maiden speech, however, was a model of decorum. The ranting and raving considered suitable for the faithful at home was toned down. Paisley appeared reasonable in his defense of the Protestant position that Ulster must irrevocably be linked to Britain. Paisley's public utterances in England have generally been moderate in tone and sometimes positively liberal. He opposed the introduction of internment in August 1971, a remarkable departure from the general Protestant line. He has indicated that he attempts to be a good member of Parliament for his Catholic constituents as well as his Protestant ones. Paisley now favors the total integration of Ulster into the United Kingdom, rather than the restoration of Stormont, or the unilateral declaration of independence favored by William Craig's Vanguard extremists.

What are Mr. Paisley's fundamental views? First and foremost, he regards Christian revelation, in its fundamentalist, Calvinist form, as the only true religion ordained by God for the salvation of mankind. All other approaches to the nature and meaning of life are in error. God has revealed Himself irrevocably and finally in the Bible and those who reject this salvific message are damned for eternity. Paisley emphasizes the necessity of man's absolute adherence to his conception of Christianity.

To Paisley, Roman Catholicism is a Satanic invention which eternally wars against true Christianity. Rome represents "another gospel" and is not a fellow Christian church. He considers the Roman Church not only theologically defective but socially and culturally pernicious, an evil system which produces an unregenerate people and a degenerate society. Hence, Paisley urges his followers to eschew fellowship with Roman Catholics and to be continually on the alert to Romanist infiltration into the cultural and political life of his beloved Ulster. "You are fighting the ancient battle of Biblical Protestantism against Popery," he told a gathering of loyalist workers.

Paisley believes that any nation which tolerates or subsidizes Romanism is in danger of Divine judgment. He heaps opprobrium on liberalism and moderate Protestantism. He regards ecumenism as a dangerous, diabolical deceit and urges true Christians to "separate" from apostate churches.

These pungent quotes from Paisley's speeches (or sermons, since it is difficult to differentiate the theological from the political) should clarify his position:

We are at war in this Province with the hierarchy of the Roman Catholic Church . . . The Jesuits are the Gestapo of the Vatican. Their purpose is to undo the Reformation and bring Protestantism and all other religions of the world under the jackboot of the Papacy . . . The hatred of all things British and Protestant is but the product of the diabolical and soul-destroying doctrines of the Church of Rome. The system that produced Hitler and Mussolini has given birth in this country to the hatemongers of Bogside . . . The I.R.A. is the armed wing of the Roman Catholic Church . . . The age-long dream of (that Church) is an Ireland Romanized from end to end, the people of God in chains or driven forever from the land of their birth. This must never happen! We must hold Ulster by every means God lays to our hands . . . Protestants of this Province must not be deceived by leading Romanists, Ecumenists, Communists, and Anarchists. Their soft words are but a Devil's lullaby to chloroform Protestantism in order that (this) Romanist-sponsored rebellion in our midst might succeed . . . The belief in the good faith of the British Government, which has sided with the Roman Catholic hierarchy against the Ulster Government, is the vapouring of minds drugged into abject subjection by the sops of an able and subtle foe. Ulster is betrayed . . . If the forces of the British Crown are going to support the I.R.A. to destroy Ulster, then we are prepared to do as our Fathers did and fight for our freedom . . . When the call comes we will be able to take our stand as Protestant men in the battle that is going to be waged . . .

Paisley is also something of an author in a curious sort of way. He wrote a book hailing the 1859 Evangelical Revival in Ulster, a commentary on the Epistle to the Romans, and a book concerning the fundamentals of Christianity. One of the strangest books I've ever seen is Paisley's *Billy Graham and The Church of Rome,* which attacks the famed American evangelist's alleged sympathies for Romanism. Paisley has always opposed Graham's inclusiveness and openness to many expressions of Christian life, and acidly criticized Graham's short visit to Ulster in 1972. Paisley's most recent work is *The St. Bartholomew's Day Massacre,* an historical account of the 1572 tragedy. Paisley is obsessed with "martyrdom" and Roman Catholic oppression of Protestants. His "Martyr's Memorial Church" is appropriately named, as it seeks to keep alive Protestant fears of a new wave of persecutions.

Paisley occasionally exhibits some coarse humor. He refers

61

to the Pope as "old Mr. Redsocks" and hints that the crumbs Roman Catholics receive from Ulster Protestant tables must be full of vitamins since the Romanists are so healthy. Paisley apparently has a well-developed olfactory sense, since he once declared that one can "smell Popery" when he crosses the border to the Irish Republic!

One should not discount Mr. Paisley's widespread influence, as he will probably be on the center stage of Ulster history for a long time to come.

No one can understand the religious aspects of the Ulster conflict unless he is aware of the fears expressed by many of the editorials from Ian Paisley's *Protestant Telegraph.* (See Appendix). I do not wish to overemphasize the strength of these views. They probably do not represent the majority Protestant view—but they do certainly represent a significantly large minority. Many of the comments strike a sympathetic chord among more moderate Protestants. It is doubtful that ultimate peace can come to Ulster unless the Protestants who subscribe to these views can be convinced that their fears are largely groundless.

I don't wish to imply that there is no Catholic bigotry. There is. But, it is directed at the Protestants more as a community rather than a religious group per se. Their hatreds are nationalistic in tone. There is very little anti-Protestantism among Catholics compared to the anti-Catholicism among many Protestants. There is a subtle twist, however. *The Catholic Truth Society* publishes incredibly simplistic pamphlets on "The One True Church." The Bishop of Down and Connor recently reiterated that his church is the one true church and that's that. This is certainly a form of bigotry and not likely to improve Protestant-Catholic relations. Dr. Farren, Roman Catholic Bishop of Londonderry, also warned Catholics against social relationships with non-Catholics. He said:

If you allow your children to be contaminated by those who are not of the fold, then you can expect nothing but disaster, and surely the disasters that have happened should be warning for you.

There is plenty of prejudice on both sides, but it takes different forms.

One of the world's most fascinating semi-secret societies is the Orange Order. Anyone who has ever seen the Order's full regalia, its orange sashes, lively music, and giant lambeg drums on the 12th of July will realize the fervent intensity with which the Order is endowed.

It is primarily a religious organization and is devoted to the maintenance of the Protestant Ascendancy in the United Kingdom. The history of the Order is somewhat murky, though it can be traced to a declaration on November 12, 1688, at Exeter Cathedral in England where William of Orange gave an address on the relationship of the Protestant religion to the government, laws, and liberties of England. Those who rallied to the Williamite cause during the three year struggle for power in England between William and James II, were the first Orangemen.

The Order itself, as a separate fraternal institution, dates from 1795, a period of agitation for Irish independence from Great Britain. It was during this period that the Battle of the Diamond occurred and the United Irishmen were founded. There were many secret societies and much mutual antagonism between Protestants and Catholics during this period. The Irish Parliament relieved Roman Catholics in 1793 from most of the penal laws and admitted them to parliamentary franchise. A full-fledged debate was soon to begin over Catholic Emancipation. The Orange Order existed primarily to defend the Protestant religion and to maintain the union between Britain and Ireland, which was officially ratified in the 1800 Act of Union.

Throughout most of the 19th Century, the Order had its ups and downs, being reactivated during periods of conflict and strife. It gained a considerable amount of strength during the

1820s when the battle over Catholic Emancipation reached its climax in 1829. When Home Rule agitation began in the late 1800s, the Orange Order gained considerable strength. After the partition of 1921, the Order became the dominant fraternal organization in Ulster and had considerable influence on the government. The Order's main concern was establishing a system of religious instruction in the schools of Ulster and maintaining Protestant control of the government. The Order has been vigilant in maintaining Ulster's independence against those who support a united Ireland. Orangemen flocked to the British armies in both World War I and II with great enthusiasm. They are truly Loyalists.

The Order is also ecumenical in the Protestant sense of bringing together individuals of all Protestant denominations. They are strongly opposed to any ecumenical overtures to the Roman Catholic Church.

In 1966 the Orange Order adopted a strong statement against ecumenism:

> The Grand Orange Lodge of Ireland views with the utmost concern the present trend towards one united church involving the surrender of our distinctive Protestant witness and the atmosphere created by the World Council of Churches to promote this goal. We deplore the compromising implications of the successive visits to the Vatican of church leaders, culminating in the recent visit of the Archbishop of Canterbury. During the past number of years there have been marked departures within the churches from the Protestant and reformed faith. We firmly believe it is now time to call for a return in our Protestant churches to the principles of the Reformation. Members of the Orange Order are pledged to love, uphold and defend the Protestant religion and are therefore called upon to resist any encroachment on their heritage regardless of the cost and consequences.

Rev. S.E. Long's essay on Orangeism in the Modern World in the book *Orangeism* states: "Any unbiased examination of Orangeism must admit that the Orange Order has provided a rallying point for Protestant men who want to champion their religion against forces and influences which would cabin and confine it. It has fought many battles within the law for the principles of Protestantism."

The Order has a prescribed ritual with a number of traditional prayers and scripture readings and the normal business of a fraternal lodge. It has great political influence and has generally been considered the power behind the throne in Ulster. It has an estimated 100,000 members in Ulster today and many members throughout the World.

To join the Orange Order, one must be a faithful Protestant, not married to a Roman Catholic and, according to the official membership requirement, not to have been born a Roman Catholic. However, when I spoke to Martin Smyth, the Grand Master of the Orange Lodge, he told me that a person converted from Roman Catholicism to Protestantism could become a member of the Orange Order. Individuals must also promise never to attend a Roman Catholic service or to in any way "countenance popish worship." "Individuals must pledge to uphold the Protestant religion and the liberties of England" in the words of the famous Williamite Settlement. The Order, in fact, has expelled members for attending Catholic services. The Order also opposed admitting Catholics to the Unionist Party in the late '50s. The Grand Master of the Orange Lodge in 1959, Sir George Clark, stated that Roman Catholics could not be admitted to the Unionist Party under any circumstances because "an Orangeman is pledged to resist, by all lawful means, the ascendancy of the Church of Rome." Paradoxically, the Order pledges to abstain from any mistreatment or uncharitable actions towards individual Roman Catholics.

The Orange Order has been severely criticized for being a negative, divisive force in Ulster and one that is hopelessly benighted. Its members see the Order as a bulwark of civil and religious liberty. The truth probably lies somewhere inbetween.

Following is a classic statement of Orange principles, written in the nineteenth century by Robert Rutledge Kane, a minister of The Church of Ireland.

65

TWENTY REASONS FOR BEING AN ORANGEMAN

1. Because I desire to live to the Glory of God, and, resisting error, superstition and idolatry, earnestly to contend for the faith once delivered to the saints.
2. Because I desire to combine with my Protestant brethren for the sake of mutual testimony, protection and love.
3. Because connection with the Orange Order draws men's attention to the history of past deliverances and arouses them to vigilance, energy and the witness for God.
4. Because I desire to remember the mercies of God, bestowed at the Reformation and also at "the glorious revolution" under William III, Prince of Orange.
5. Because an Orangeman is bound to show faith by his life, his desire for man's salvation, his obedience to the dictates of Protestantism and his efforts to deliver Romanists from mental perversion and spiritual slavery.
6. Because the members of the Orange Institution have always been enabled by the Grace of God to exhibit loyalty, patience, firmness and brotherly love.
7. Because Orangemen honour the Holy Bible at all their meetings, conduct their proceedings by its heavenly precepts and form the Orange Ritual chiefly from its sublime prophecy.
8. Because the empire has always flourished when Protestant leaders guided the helm of state by the light of God's revealed will and when Protestant truths were in the supremacy.
9. Because I learn by the doctrines, history and daily practices of the Church of Rome that the lives of Protestants are endangered, the laws of England set at nought and the Crown of England subordinated to the dictation of an Italian bishop.
10. Because the Papacy has never repented and cannot repent of its continental massacres of Protestants, of its demon Inquisitions and Irish rebellions of 1641 and 1798.

11. Because Popery annually breathes denunciations at Rome by a well-known "Bull" against the existence of heretics, otherwise Protestants.
12. Because the Church of Rome teaches in her schools that heresy is not to be endured nor heretics permitted to live.
13. Because Popery is not content with equality and because it claims the unconstitutional privilege of a double allegiance to the Pope and Queen, also the right of her priests to withhold treasonable and felonious communications and for the Pope to be arbiter of the lives, laws and liberties of mankind.
14. Because notwithstanding the private worth of many members of the Romish Church, that generally Roman Catholic jurymen refuse to give a true verdict according to evidence when the cause of their Church or Party is at stake.
15. Because Popery maintains a continual rancour against the Protestant people of Great Britain, receiving their charities with ingratitude and stimulating its followers to detest the Saxon and to loathe rule and realm of England.
16. Because Jesuits are openly tolerated in Great Britain and Ireland, contrary to the express laws of the Empire.
17. Because all truckling to Popery has, in every instance, been attended with renewed clamour for further concessions in violation of pledges given by Roman Catholics.
18. Because it cannot be otherwise, but that under the downward progress of British legislation, God will be made angry and the nation imperilled. Protestant union and testimony are therefore required to deprecate God's indignation and to bide the time of needful resistance.
19. Because many who were Romanists have been led by the vigour and fidelity of Protestant testimony to contrast it with their unholy bondage system and to forsake it by God's blessing forever.
20. Because the whole history of the Bible assures us that, if we are prayerful, united and zealous for God, the Time, the Man and the Deliverance will come.

Anthem. The tune is "What a Friend We Have in Jesus."

ULSTER VANGUARD ANTHEM

Stand together, men of Ulster!
  Stand together, side by side!
Let no envy mar your Union,
  Let no jealousy divide.
Put away misunderstanding,
  Trust each other heart and soul;
Till the morn of peace is dawning,
  And the clouds asunder roll.

Stand together, men of Ulster!
  Look to God to guard His own;
He is watching all your movements,
  His right arm is round you thrown.
He will scatter all the danger,
  Changing trouble into peace;
Trust your cause to God Almighty,
  And the tempest soon will cease.

"No Surrender!" men of Ulster!
  Till the peril pass away,
Man the walls of truth and freedom,
  Trust in God, and watch and pray.
Forward, in the cause of Vanguard;
  Trust in God, and plan and do.
Look! the banner floats above you:
  The same that o'er your fathers flew.

5.   Educational Apartheid

> "Education will always be a thorny
> problem in the Province, for no single thing has
> contributed more to disharmony among the
> people . . . . No study of Irish history can begin
> to make sense until this primary fact is
> appreciated."
>   Rev. S.E. Long, *Orangeism* (1967)

One of the basic roots of the Ulster conflict is the system of
almost total religious segregation in the educational process. In
1961 only 879 out of 90,000 Catholic students attended the
state-run school system, while 101,728 out of 103,000 Protestant pupils attended public schools. Thus, until university
(which only a tiny percentage of Ulster citizens ever attend) or
occupational experience, Catholic and Protestant young people
never have an opportunity to develop meaningful friendships or
social relations.

Under the 1921 Government of Ireland Act, responsibility
for education was given to the Stormont Parliament by London.
Three basic kinds of schools exist. The county schools, under
the direction of each county or borough council operating as the
local education authority, are the public schools theoretically
provided for all children. They are "wholly maintained" by the
government. Most Protestant schools voluntarily transferred to

69

this system in 1923. The "voluntary maintained" schools, mostly Catholic, are run by a six-member board, four from the schools' managers and two from the local education authority. These schools qualify for more generous government grants and appear to be the ideal relationship for the church authorities. Here they can have their cake and eat it too. The "non-maintained" voluntary schools are completely under church control but still receive public grants which are generous by American standards. One of the anomalies of the educational financing system is that Section 5 of the Government of Ireland Act prohibits the endowment of any religion. Due to typical British inability to understand church-state separation, however, this principle was never applied to the church-run schools.

Latest educational data reveal that 111,064 students attend the county primary schools compared to 101,055 for the voluntary schools. On the secondary level (age 11 to 16), a majority attend the voluntary schools. The "grammar" schools, which are more academic in nature, educate 39,083 pupils in the voluntary system compared to 12,559 in the county system.

The grammar schools provide a seven-year course after age 11, or the fifth year of ordinary primary schooling. A few grammar schools have their own preparatory academies. They are fee-charging schools, but more than 80 percent of the pupils hold local education authority scholarships. Ulster, incidentally, has a very impressive scholarship system for both secondary grammar schools and the universities. Very few deserving but poor children are denied an education, unlike many other countries in the world.

The grammar schools are diverse in origin. Some were established by Royal Charter, some on the model of Scottish academies or English public schools, and some by church authorities or religious orders. There are 81 recognized grammar schools in Ulster today; 21 are county schools under local education authorities while 60 are voluntary schools, 34 Protestant and 26 Catholic.

The "secondary intermediate" schools educate 45,786 students in the county schools compared to 38,757 in the voluntary schools. Almost half of Ulster's children (158,000 out of 352,000) attend Roman Catholic schools, though the Roman Catholic population is estimated at 35 percent of the total. The high Catholic birthrate, 28.3 per 1,000 compared to 20.0 for Protestants, is largely responsible for this phenomenon.

The Catholic schools have always received generous funding from the Protestant Unionist government. The direct grants were increased from 50 percent to 65 percent and in April 1968 to 80 percent. Thus, if a new Catholic school is to be built, the local educational authority pays 80 percent of the building costs for the "maintained" schools. "Non-maintained" schools still receive a 65 percent direct grant. The vast majority of Roman Catholic schools have decided to accept the "maintained" status. It is also significant that the local educational people (two of the six committee members) have no control over the internal running of the schools. The concept of public accountability does not apply here. Local government pays 100 percent of external maintenance costs for the Catholic schools, plus 100 percent of the teachers' salaries. This is done despite the fact that many of the Roman Catholic teachers are not certified by the Northern Ireland Ministry of Education, having been trained by religious orders in the Republic. Even the "non-maintained" Catholic schools receive 65 percent of all internal and external maintenance and alteration costs. The government pays for 65 percent of all lunch and milk costs in "non-maintained" Catholic schools and 80 percent of these costs for the "maintained" ones.

The law provides that the local educational authorities may provide for transportation to and from school or pay traveling expenses in whole or in part for these schools. Whatever else may be said about discrimination in housing, jobs, or political rights, the Roman Catholic school system receives 95 percent of its total budget costs from the government. Incidentally, the Northern Ireland government spends

71

twice as much per capita on education as the 95 percent Catholic Republic of Ireland to the south.

Virtually the only area in which integrated education occurs is the handful of vocation-technical schools and the universities. Catholics participate fully in the programs at Queens University and make up 22 percent of the student body. State scholarships are granted without religious preference. However, there are only 10,000 university students in Ulster out of 1,525,000 people.

Separatism in education extends to the teaching staff. The Ministry of Education operates Stanmillis College, which is nondenominational but in reality Protestant, since the Roman Catholic church operates its own teaching training colleges. The Catholic colleges are still segregated by sex, in line with the extreme social conservatism of Irish Catholicism. St. Mary's College trains female lay teachers, while St. Joseph's trains the males. The main religious order responsible for Roman Catholic education in Ulster is the Christian Brothers. All three teacher training colleges are part of Queens University's Institute of Education. Protestants belong to the Ulster Teachers Union while Catholics support the Irish National Teachers organization.

Why do Ulster Catholics insist on separate education so strenuously? After all, straight religious instruction can occur in many settings, not just during school hours. If integration were to come in education, the Catholic clergy would have rights of access and could teach religious doctrine at prescribed times, as the Protestant clergy do in many schools now. Perhaps a real underlying reason is revealed by Sister Mary Laurentia, Vice Principal of St. Dominic's Roman Catholic grammar school in Belfast. In an interview with the *Christian Science Monitor* (September 12, 1969), she stated that Catholics must retain their schools in order to provide a total "Catholic attitude" for the children of their faith. They want the freedom, she implied, to bring out the Catholic point of view in all school subjects so that it permeates the entire school life of the child.

72

And all at government expense! Incidentally, Catholic schools refuse to fly the nation's flag (the Union Jack) or to sing the National Anthem. On November 20, 1972 they refused to declare a holiday in honor of the Queen's 20th Coronation Anniversary. Catholic schools in England, Wales and Scotland closed.

How adequate are Catholic schools educationally? No objective survey has ever been conducted by the Ministry of Education. However, some critics charge that the Catholic school system is inferior and does not prepare its students to cope with many of the complexities of modern society. Though almost 50 percent of school children in Ulster are Catholic, only 20 percent of Queens University students are Catholic. Stephen Preston, writing in the *London Daily Telegraph* May 7, 1969, states that many Catholic schools "remain outdated, over-crowded and far below the level of comparable state schools in the same area. The Roman Catholic hierarchy," he charges, "has placed its people under a series of disadvantages because of its insistence on the attendance of Catholic children only at Catholic schools. The disproportionately small number of Roman Catholics 'at the top' in Ulster can well be ascribable to other causes than pure Protestant malice."

Who is responsible for this tragic division in Ulster's educational institutions? The blame must be shared by the churches themselves. During the 19th century both religions insisted on separate denominational education as a method of insuring loyalty and control over their adherents. The Catholic bishops fiercely opposed attempts to establish an integrated state educational system in 1831-35 and again in the crucial 1919-23 period.

The Roman Catholics refused to work with the Lynn com-mittee, established by the new government in 1922 to examine all phases of education in Northern Ireland. The committee recommended establishment of a system of primary education for all children. The Education Act of 1923 provided that all existing denominational schools be transferred to the local

73

education authorities, forbade religious instruction during school hours, and declared that the religion of a teacher was not considered a factor in appointment.

The far-sighted Minister of Education, Lord Londonderry, genuinely believed in integrated education and opposed the introduction of religious divisiveness into the new school system. Unfortunately, the Protestant churches and the Grand Orange Lodge attacked the provisions and formed United Education Committees to fight for Bible instruction in the schools. Eventually, amendments passed in 1925 and in 1930 restored religious instruction to the schools for a half hour each day. If ten or more parents in each school desired it, it became the duty of the education authority to provide Bible instruction, taught by the teachers from an agreed syllabus. The Protestant churches received a minimum of 50 percent representation on all local education committees. Heated controversy concerning religious instruction and the religious affiliation of the teachers continued well into the 1940s. Throughout this dispute, the Catholic church insisted on its own separate system. The Protestant schools gradually transferred to the state system. Both sides generally remained satisfied with this system, since it effectively helped to perpetuate the communal divisions.

In 1947 the act was amended to excuse teachers who did not wish to participate in the religious program. In some communities, local clergymen taught the religious courses. Today the law reads: "The school day begins in county and voluntary schools with a collective act of worship unless circumstances make it impracticable. Religious instruction, which must be given in these schools, is undenominational in county schools but in voluntary schools its nature is determined by the managers. In county schools teachers may be excused from attendance at or participation in the religious exercise and parents of children who wish them to be wholly or partly excused from either the collective act of worship or religious instruction in any school may have them excused; if these rights are exercised neither teachers nor children may suffer any disadvantage. The collective act of worship and the religious instruction must be so arranged that every school, whether county or voluntary, is open to pupils of all religious denominations for instruction other than religious instruction and that no pupil may be excluded directly or indirectly from the other advantages which the school affords." An agreed syllabus attempts to provide guidelines for religious education. This system is essentially the same as in England and Wales.

An examination of the syllabus used in Ulster's state schools reveals no explicit anti-Catholic bias. It was drawn up by representatives of the Presbyterian, Methodist and Anglican (Church of Ireland) churches. It is billed as nondenominational. However, it is hardly that. It is nondenominational only in the sense that it doesn't take sides between Presbyterians, Methodists and Anglicans! It does reflect a strong orientation toward the Reformed theology expressed in the Westminster Confession of Faith and The Thirty Nine Articles. It would be totally inappropriate for a pluralistic society which reflects diverse theological viewpoints. In fact, outside of the three churches mentioned, it is hard to see how other Christians would appreciate the course used in Ulster's public schools.

The course does not examine the history of Christianity in much detail. It jumps from the first to the twentieth century with great rapidity. Other world religions are not mentioned, though it is suggested as an afterthought that the students might profit from an examination of the insights of other great world religions. The literary aspects of the Bible are not considered. No religion course in a public school would ever satisfy everybody, but this one has more than its share of gaps.

It defines the Lord's Day as the "first day of the week, Resurrection Day, or Sunday," which would offend Seventh-day Adventists. It refers to the "Two Sacraments of the New Testament," which would offend not only those who believe in seven sacraments (Roman Catholics, Greek Orthodox and High Episcopalians) but those who prefer the theological term "ordinances" (Baptists). The course states: "bishops, deacons,

75

and presbyters are mentioned in later New Testament writing, but it is not clear whether they were separate orders." This would offend those who believe in apostolic succession and a threefold historic ministry. The syllabus refers to the Lord's Supper as a "memorial" which would violate the consciences of those who believe in the Real Presence or other interpretations of the meaning of this service.

In another rather explicit doctrinal statement, the syllabus states: "When we look at the history of the Church we find that at the times of great danger the Holy Spirit has moved through theological reformations and the moral purification of the church." It is hard to see how Unitarian and Jewish children (and there are a few thousand in Ulster) could be expected to participate fully in this "nondenominational" religion course.

Though the syllabus claims not to proselytize, one wonders what the following passage really means: "Though it is not the responsibility of the school to lead pupils into active church membership and personal commitment, it is one of the tasks of religious education to show that Christian living is incomplete without personal commitment, and one of the outward expressions of this is membership in the church."

I have reproduced below the table of contents and statement of purpose for the "religious education" course in Ulster's secondary state-run schools.

God was in Christ

A handbook for teachers on the first year of the syllabus of religious education for secondary schools.

INTRODUCTION

The Christian Faith is the conviction that this world, among the immensities of the universe, is no mere accident. Kindness, courage, self-sacrifice and other great and noble things of life are not merely human ideals in an indifferent environment. The order and beauty of the world and the strivings of the human heart derive from a living God who

77

has made His mind and purpose clear to those who have ears to hear and eyes to see. In God's providential governing of the world it was the Hebrew people who, over a period of more than a thousand years, learned more clearly than others to see His hand in history and to hear His voice in their hearts.

The culmination of this experience came through the life and teaching of Jesus. In Him men met One who spoke with unusual authority about God, who set before them the true way of life and lived it Himself in kindness, courage and truth. They saw Him resisting the common temptations of men to self-indulgence and self-aggrandisement, defeating the power of evil in His own life and in His environment. At the height of His powers they saw Him going to death willingly for the sake of His people. Through these acts and words His followers saw the power of God and came to recognise Jesus as the Son of God, God incarnate, true God and true man. In Him God has actually fulfilled His promises to the Hebrew people for the benefit of all mankind. Jesus came to rescue men and reconcile them with God.

The course therefore attempts:

(1) To make a vivid presentation of the historical Jesus as a real man living a full human life.

(2) To call forth a personal response and commitment to Him as God Incarnate.

(3) To set Jesus' life in the context of Jewish history, customs and tradition.

(4) To show the relevance of the Gospel to some personal and social problems of today.

It is assumed that each of the thirty-one topics will provide enough material for at least a week's lessons. Where the accounts in St. Matthew, St. Mark and St. Luke are closely parallel, St. Mark, as the oldest Gospel record, is quoted.

We begin the course with the central New Testament convictions that Jesus our Lord suffered for us and having risen from the dead, is our living Master. The first three sections will deal with the Crucifixion, the Resurrection and the circumstances in which they occurred.

Jesus the King

A handbook for teachers on the second year of the syllabus of religious education for secondary schools

PREFACE

The second year of the Syllabus continues the general aim of the first year, namely, to help teachers to present to their pupils (i) the centrality of Jesus Christ for the Christian faith as the One Who is supremely relevant now and Who demands personal response and commitment from those who call themselves Christians; (ii) that the Word of God found in the Bible is always contemporary and relevant to personal, national, and international life; (iii) the essential unity of the Bible; (iv) the fruits of modern Biblical scholarship, and (v) the necessary background material in order that the Biblical narrative may be understood in its context. The notes should be read with the above aims in mind for they have been prepared on the assumption that teachers having studied them will choose suitable methods of presentation and adapt the material where necessary to suit the interests and abilities of their classes. (Suggestions on Method can be found in an appendix in the First Year Notes.)

Here it may be pointed out that each section provides

sufficient material for a week's work of four lessons, but each teacher must utilize the sections in relation to the level of ability of his class. Thus if a section becomes the basis of a Project a class may spend a month on it, whereas in another case a section may be dealt with in a single lesson. The actual syllabus taught will, as already indicated, depend on the nature of the class being taught for what is presented here is intended as a guide and aid to the teacher and not a straight-jacket. In fact it is hoped that teachers will experiment in presenting the material to classes, but in every case it is essential that the aims of the Course as set out above and at the beginning of the first year be understood so that it can make its maximum impact.

Where a class is below average ability it is suggested that the teacher make a careful choice of the sections in order to make a coherent course, keeping in mind the necessity to present to the pupils the centrality of Jesus Christ and the relevance of His teaching for their lives. With these classes it is of special value to link up lessons with specific Christian activities going on outside the school so that terms like "service" and "loving our neighbour as ourselves" take on a concrete meaning.

Certain sections lend themselves to the discussion technique, but at this age it is suggested that this should not be overdone. The Bible is the book which sets forth the facts upon which our faith is based. We cannot expect anyone to enter into the experience of the first disciples unless they know the story of Jesus. His teaching and the early Church as it is told in the Gospels, the Acts and the Epistles set against the background of the history of Israel as we have it in the Old Testament. That is why there is much Biblical narrative given and because the notes are for teachers they have an academic approach, though there are hints as to the presentation. Yet it is not forgotten that Christianity is equally a living relationship with the God and Father of our Lord Jesus Christ, a quality of life which can only be lived by those who share the mind and spirit of Jesus. It is one of the great problems of Christian Education as to how to hold these two aspects in a right balance in the presentation of the Christian faith to young people.

One of the issues raised in respect of the above is the question of memory or repetition work. This is of value with certain classes but it is difficult to prescribe passages for this age-group and therefore teachers are left free to choose passages which they think will effectively sum up the aim of their lessons.

Finally, it would be of great value if the theme of the School Assembly Prayers was related, whenever possible, to themes found in the Syllabus so that learning could be in the context of praise and worship which is the most effective context.

Prophet, Priest and King

A handbook for teachers on the third and fourth years of the syllabus of religious education for secondary intermediate, technical and comprehensive schools.

PREFACE

The publication of this course in Religious Education marks the completion of a syllabus for secondary schools covering more than three school years. Because it has taken a relatively long time to produce, and because it has had to be issued in three parts, the unity of the syllabus and the principles guiding the syllabus committee have sometimes become obscured. It is appropriate, therefore, at this stage to comment on the syllabus as a whole.

Traditionally committees preparing syllabuses in religious education have thought in terms of fairly distinct Old Testament and New Testament sections. The aim of the present committee has been to make the person and teaching of Christ central and to relate themes, stories and teaching found in the Old Testament to the New Testament message of redemption. In a broad sense each of the courses has been addressed to one of three fundamental questions:

First year: Who was Jesus?

Second year: What did He do?

Third and fourth years: What did He teach and what resulted from His life and teaching?

These questions are posed at the climax of Jesus' life on earth and the answers are found in His life and teaching, in the history of His people, and in the witness of His church. In the first year Jesus is seen as a member of a race claiming a special relationship with God. This relationship, and its origins and development in history, are then given significance in the context of His ministry. Concurrently an attempt is made to show the relevance of His life, with its concerns and priorities, to our individual lives and to the life of society.

In the second year Jesus' proclamation of the Kingdom of God is central. The syllabus aims to show that an understanding of His Kingship depends on knowledge of Old Testament kings: its emphasis is equally on the meaning of His reign in the world of today.

The present course views Jesus' teaching in the light of the prophetic tradition. Prophets chosen are those whose concern for righteousness is reflected in Jesus' ministry, and whose message is particularly relevant to the twentieth century. There is a separate section on areas of life in which young people can exercise the kind of responsibility demanded by the prophets and by 'one greater than a

84

prophet'. The course also includes a considerable amount of material which although it does not arise directly out of the prophetic theme is yet allied to it. The life of the church is life in the 'new covenant' in Christ proclaimed by the Prophets and the function of the church is to witness to the continuing power of the Resurrection. The committee thought it necessary to deal specifically with the 'Church and the Sacraments' so as to fulfill the purposes of the syllabus as a whole, to help teachers to present to their pupils Jesus Christ as the One who is supremely relevant now and Who demands personal response and commitment from those who call themselves Christians.

It has been emphasised at meetings of teachers and ministers throughout the province that the courses as set out are for the teacher; the material included is to help him to achieve the objectives of sound religious education. Everywhere the teacher has the responsibility of selecting and adapting material with the needs of particular children in mind since there is appropriate material for pupils of differing levels of ability. Both A and C streams can find answers to the questions around which the various years are built: the differences are of depth and range of understanding rather than of involvement and response.

Because of the historic interfaith tensions in Ulster, which the schools reflect, there is the very real problem of presenting the opposing religion and its adherents in a positive light. No systematic analysis has tackled this subject, but Denis Barritt and Charles Carter commented in their book *The Northern Ireland Problem,* "We have had numerous complaints from both sides of derogatory and slanderous teachings about the other group, imparted in the classroom. These complaints are usually vague, but some are no doubt justified."

The possibility of a changing Catholic approach toward segregated education seems remote though Cardinal Conway,

Ireland's Primate, did indicate in 1971 that he was "considering" the possibility that integrated education may someday be acceptable. Conway's 1970 pamphlet *Catholic Education* reiterates the Church's insistence on separate education.

Catholic intransigence on the education question is truly dismaying. When the new town of Craigavon was established a few years ago, Catholic and Protestant families chose to live next door to each other—one of the few areas in Ulster where housing is not segregated. However, the Roman Catholic Church insisted on separate education and even playground facilities. Another opportunity for harmony was lost. There is evidence that many Catholics reject their church's position on sectarian education. Professor Richard Rose's 1967 survey showed that a whopping 69 percent of Catholics endorsed integrated education. Unfortunately, they are subservient to the clergy's wishes. The spirit of Catholic revolt, so evident in Holland and the United States, hasn't yet reached the Emerald Isle. The hierarchy points out that even the supposedly progressive Second Vatican Council issued a Declaration on Christian Education which reaffirmed the value of a specifically Catholic education, preferably at government expense.

What do many informed observers think about segregated education in Ulster? Are Americans who believe in church-state separation the only critics of this approach to education? Hardly. The respected London *Economist* commented in July 1971: "Education is probably the biggest single source of Ulster's growing social division. By underwriting segregation through separate schools for Catholics, the Unionists . . . kept the two communities permanently apart . . . The Catholic hierarchy should think again about the obstinate stand it takes on education, for it is in the schools and playgrounds that Protestant and Catholic children could learn that faith is not a barrier to friendship."

G.W. Target wrote in *Unholy Smoke,* "The Roman Catholic insistence on separate schools almost invariably leads

86

to both sections of the community growing up in ignorance or prejudice of each other . . . . We are breeding generations of bigots." The World Alliance of Reformed Churches concluded that "the system of confessionally based education so sharply separating the communities should be abolished."

Another view is expressed by the Minority Rights Group, a human rights and civil liberties research organization in London. They concluded in *The Two Irelands:* "The root cause of the difficulties has been in education. The Catholic hierarchy, as in many other counties, has insisted that its flock be taught in Catholic schools. This has meant that from the age of five years the two communities have led separate lives in the most formative area. They do not see one another, they are taught different aspects of their joint history, they inherit different cultural outlooks . . . In spite of pressure, not least from the Catholics, that this system should be ended in favor of integrated education, the Roman Catholic Church has remained intransigent. Like many another exiled community— and this is in essence how it sees itself—it has a horror that unless its tenets are rigidly inculcated into its adherents they will gradually succumb to the mores of the major group."

Dr. Morris Fraser, an eminent Belfast psychiatrist, warns that "while segregation of school children continues, episodes of community strife in Ireland will recur throughout, and probably beyond, the foreseeable future." Captain William J. Long, Northern Ireland's former Minister of Education, sees religious segregation in education as "a great pity." It is bound to accentuate differences between Catholics and Protestants," he said. "The formative attitudes acquired in the school years stick throughout life."

When I spoke to former Prime Minister Terence O'Neill in London, he reiterated what he said at an ecumenical conference in Corrymeela, April 8, 1966: "A major cause of division arises, some would say, from the *de facto* segregation along religious lines. This is a most delicate matter and one must respect the firm conditions from which it springs. Many people have questioned, however, whether the maintenance of two distinct educational systems side by side is not wasteful of human and financial resources, and a major barrier to communal understanding." Even this delicate comment invoked the opprobrium of Cardinal Conway.

Some strong Catholic voices have, however, been added to the list of advocates of integration. These include Dr. Garret Fitzgerald, the Irish Republic's new Minister for Foreign Affairs; Rev. Michael Harley, director of the Irish School of Ecumenics in Dublin; and Rev. Michael McGreil, lecturer in sociology at St. Patrick's College, Maynooth. All are from the Republic. Father McGreil was quoted in *Religious News Service* May 31, 1973 as stating: "If we had the courage to set about building our communities through a common educational structure or system, I believe we would be well on the way to building a new Ireland."

It might be worth recalling that a far-sighted 19th century Catholic bishop, James W. Doyle of Kildare, defended mutual education in an eloquent statement. "I do not know of any measure which would prepare the way for a better feeling in Ireland than uniting children at an early age, and bringing them up in the same school, leading them to commune with one another and to form those little initmacies and friendships which often subsist through life."

Some organizations which recently endorsed integrated education include: National Council of Civil Liberties, Northern Ireland Civil Rights Association, The Cameron Commission Report, the Catholic Renewal Movement, Official Sinn Fein, the Republican Clubs, the Belfast Humanist Group, the Alliance Party, Northern Ireland Labour Party, the *Belfast Telegraph,* the Ulster Teacher's Union (Protestant;, and the Irish National Teachers Organization (Catholic). Since the redoubtable member of Parliament for Mid-Ulster, Bernadette Devlin, is something of an institution, we can add her to the list.

A solid two-thirds of Ulstermen and women favored

integration in the 1967 Loyalty Poll. In May 1973 the *Fortnight* poll shown below indicated an even heavier majority. Further analysis of the poll's results revealed that only the supporters of Ian Paisley and the Provisional IRA were against integration!

Integrated Education

Q. How would you feel about your children, or children you know, going to school attended by pupils and taught by teachers some of whom were Catholic and some Protestant?

	All	Protestant	Roman Catholic
Strongly in favour	31%	28%	34%
In favour	31%	31%	30%
Don't mind/willing to accept	24%	25%	21%
Against	10%	10%	10%
Strongly against	3%	3%	3%

Published in Fortnight
21st May, 1973

Almost everyone with whom I spoke in Ulster expressed a wish that integrated education, where students of both faiths could study together and develop lasting friendships, would someday become a reality. In light of Ulster's tragic history, I believe that religious integration of education in Northern Ireland is imperative.

Unfortunately, there is not much immediate hope for school integration in Ulster. Some observers feel it may be fifty years before such a policy is introduced. There is some integration in sports, the arts and the youth orchestras. The five new Education Area Boards include representatives of both school systems. Two of the forty preschool recreation centers are integrated. Only about six of the 1,500 or so schools in Ulster are significantly integrated. The Vere Foster primary school in Ballymurphy has integrated both the teaching staff and the student body, largely as a result of changing housing patterns. Though the previously mentioned polls indicate strong support for integration in principle, the 1973 White Paper sounded a cautionary note: ". . . it is by no means to be assumed that, in practice, all Protestant parents would be happy to see a completely integrated school system, involving as it would the teaching of Protestant children by Roman Catholic teachers, some of them members of religious orders." Obviously, the struggle for integration will take courage and patience.

6.   The Other Side of the Border

Do Ulster Protestants have legitimate concerns about the possibility of their future absorption into a United Ireland? Will they lose vital religious or civil liberties? Is their fear justified in the light of contemporary Irish church-state practice? For an answer to these fundamentally important questions, let's look at religion and politics in the Irish Republic.

On paper, Ireland is a model of constitutional propriety in guaranteeing the free exercise of religion, insuring nondiscrimination in religious matters by the state and guaranteeing opportunity for participation in the political life of the nation without religious favor. The 1922 Constitution prohibited religious endowments and preferences and guaranteed full religious liberty to all religions. "Freedom of conscience and the free profession and practice of religion are, subject to public order and morality, guaranteed to every citizen," the Constitution proclaimed. The "subject to public order" phrase concerned some observers but it has rarely been invoked against religious dissenters. The document guaranteed distribution of public funds to both Protestant and Catholic schools, on an equal basis, which pleased Protestants. (Some Americans would question whether this is not a sectarian endowment, but British and Irish practice, unfortunately, tend to regard religious schools as quasi-public and not subject to provisions against public funds for religious institutions.)

The 1922 Constitution did not enshrine Catholic dogma on education, marriage, birth control, censorship or divorce in the civil law. The 1937 revision of the Constitution, however, employed more sectarian bias.

The Preamble to the 1937 Constitution proclaims:

> In the name of the Most Holy Trinity, from Whom is all authority and to Whom, as our final end, all actions of both men and States must be referred,
> We, the people of Eire,
> Humbly acknowledging all our obligations to our
> Divine Lord, Jesus Christ, Who sustained our fathers through centuries of trial . . .

Article 6 declared that "all powers of government, legislative executive and judicial, derive under God from the people," which reflects Pope Leo XIII's teaching that all sovereignty comes from God, with the Catholic Church serving as divine arbiter of that sovereignty.

The most explicitly religious declarations in the new Constitution are contained in Article 44, Sections 1-3, which state:

1. The State acknowledges that the homage of public worship is due to Almighty God. It shall hold His Name in reverence, and shall respect and honour religion.
2. The State recognizes the special position of the Holy Catholic Apostolic and Roman Church as the guardian of the Faith professed by the great majority of the citizens.
3. The State also recognizes the Church of Ireland, the Presbyterian Church in Ireland, the Methodist Church in Ireland, the Religious Society of Friends of Ireland, as well as the Jewish congregations and the other religious denominations existing in Ireland at the date of the coming into operation of this Constitution.

Section 2 has been a point of contention since 1937, and many critics believe this has given the Catholic Church a preferential position, indirectly at least, in Irish society. In what was interpreted as a gesture to Ulster Protestants, the Irish Parliament, with the support of most Roman Catholic ecclesiastics, provided a referendum on whether to abolish Section 2 in December 1972.

Removal was ratified by 85 percent of the electorate. However, less than 50 percent of the eligible voters participated in this referendum, the lowest turnout on any referendum question in the Irish Republic's history. The widespread disinterest may have indicated a foregone conclusion of passage, an ambivalence among many voters, or a feeling that the question was relatively insignificant anyway.

Article 44, Section 2, paragraphs 2 and 3 are good guarantees of religious liberty:

2. The State guarantees not to endow any religion.
3. The State shall not impose any disabilities or make any discrimination on the ground of religious profession, belief or status.

Two additional articles were added to the Constitution which sullied the nonsectarianism of the original document. Article 41 bans divorce for all Irish citizens, Catholic and non-Catholic. This article is replete with pious phrases about the indissolubility of marriage, the sanctity of the family, etc. Divorce obtained in another country is not even recognized under Irish law. This places Ireland at variance with almost every civilized modern democracy and leads to moral hypocrisy. What is especially galling is the imposition of Catholic morality on the non-Catholic sector of population.

Article 40 is an ambivalent article which has been used as the basis for Ireland's infamous censorship. It states:

.... the State shall endeavour to ensure that organs of public opinion, such as the radio, the press, the cinema, while preserving their rightful liberty of expression, including criticism of government policy, shall not be used to undermine public order or morality or the authority of the State. The publication or utterance of blasphemous, seditious, or indecent matter is an offense which shall be punishable in accordance with law.

The problem arises when "morality" or "blaspheny" are

interpreted in light of Catholic doctrine.

There is no Concordat between Ireland and the Vatican, probably because one was never considered necessary. The Church, as we shall see, has immense informal power in all areas of Irish life. There is diplomatic representation with the Vatican, as expected of most Catholic countries, and the Apostolic Nuncio is dean of the diplomatic corps in Dublin. Clergy do not seek public office, and the church is officially neutral between the three major political parties (perhaps as Noel Browne suggests, because she controls all three). The church has exercised little direct influence on Irish foreign policy, though some pressure was exerted against recognizing Soviet Russia. Interestingly, a group of pro-Fascist "Blue Shirts" denounced the DeValera government for continuing to recognize the Spanish Republic during the Spanish Civil War. A legion of Blue Shirts actually fought on Franco's side in the Civil War. In short, church and state co-exist separately but in practice collaborate in certain spheres.

Let it be stated that the tiny Protestant community, which represents 130,000 out of Ireland's 2.9 million people, or slightly less than 5 percent, has always participated in Irish political, cultural, and social life. Irish nationalism has always benefited from such Protestant support as Wolfe Tone, Robert Emmett, and Charles Stewart Parnell. The first President of the Irish Republic, Douglas Hyde, was a Protestant. There has always been at least one Protestant in the Cabinet and there are four Protestants in the Dail (Parliament) out of 144. (There should be seven, however, if representation were proportional.) There are Protestant judges and civil servants, and the Lord Mayor of Dublin in the 1950s, Mr. Briscoe, was a Jew. The Deputy Prime Minister for many years, Mr. Erskine Childers, is a Protestant, as are two of the twelve top judges in the country.

Mr. Childers, 68, Ireland's leading Protestant, was elected President of the Republic on May 31, 1973, by 636,162 votes to Thomas O'Higgins' 587,577. His victory was regarded as an upset since Childers represents the conservative Fianna Fail

94

Party, which was ousted in the February parliamentary elections. His victory has to be regarded as a personal triumph and, in some ways, a gesture of conciliation toward Ulster Protestants. Childers favors Irish unity but has condemned the IRA. His father, Robert Erskine Childers—a writer and English naval officer, fought beside Eamon de Valera in the Easter Rising of 1916. He was executed during the Civil War in 1922.

Childers, born in England, is an Anglican and does not speak a word of Gaelic. He became a naturalized Irish citizen in 1938, was educated at Trinity College, and has had 35 years of experience as a Cabinet Minister and member of Parliament. His second wife is a Catholic.

The Irish President's duties are largely ceremonial and non-political. He receives heads of state and other dignitaries, signs legislation and accepts and confirms the resignations and appointments of the government.

It was felt that many liberal Catholics believed it to be the "right thing" to vote for Mr. Childers. It is certainly a propaganda boon to the Republic. Already Catholics are using this as a propaganda device. For example, the Philadelphia *Catholic Standard and Times,* June 7, 1973, commented in a lead editorial "Emerald Ecumenism":

Last week's election in the Republic of Ireland gave graphic evidence that Irish voters judge a man not by his creed but by his credentials.

An English-born Protestant, Erskine Childers, was chosen for the presidency of the Irish republic by an electorate which is more than 95 percent Catholic.

The first president of Ireland, chosen under the constitution adopted in the mid-1930s, was also a Protestant, Douglas Hyde, and Dublin's most famous Lord Mayor was a Jew, Robert Briscoe.

Narrow denominationalism is thus not a factor in elections in the Republic of Ireland—and the choice of a Protestant member of the minority party over a Catholic candidate backed by the government coalition is a tribute to

95

both the independence and fairness of the Irish electorate. The election, of course, takes on special significance at a time when the six counties of Northern Ireland are torn by tragic religious conflict. The experience of the overwhelmingly Catholic Republic of Ireland proves that Protestants are not and never have been excluded from the full benefits of Irish citizenship; Northern Ireland's Catholic minority, however, has suffered severe economic and political inequity because of religious discrimination by the Protestant majority in that small corner of the United Kingdom.

It can only be hoped that the lesson of Ireland's south will be learned in Ireland's north—that citizens of all faiths can live together in harmony when the sour note of bigotry is removed from men's laws and from men's lives.

However, another view is expressed by Dennis Kennedy, writing in the lively intellectual journal *Fortnight* (May 21, 1973):

One factor that has not been an issue at all is Mr. Childer's religion. He is a Protestant, or to be more precise, an Anglican. But there is nothing "Protestant" about Mr. Childer's politics. He is an adamant opponent of the secular state, of the permissive, even the liberal society. He has often expressed the view that Irish society, whatever it's defects, is superior to any other around!

Mr. Childer's election is impressive, but a more dramatic event would be the election of a Protestant Prime Minister some day. Hopefully Mr. Childers will be able to achieve what he stated, shortly after his election: "I would like to use whatever influence I have in establishing a sort of common feeling between the two parts of the country, and above all, in helping the two communities in the North to get to know each other better and understand each other's problems and views."

It should be considered praiseworthy that Catholics, after centuries of British and Protestant persecution in Ireland, did not retaliate directly or explicitly after the Free State was established. The memory of the Penal laws and the famine are burdens which still affect Protestant-Catholic relations in Ireland.

The 130,000 Protestants in the Republic are relatively secure economically. They are in large part the descendants of the Anglo-Irish Ascendancy. Protestants are well represented in the business and professional (banking and insurance) communities and the civil service. Six and one-half percent of the Protestants are in directorial or managerial positions compared with one percent of the Catholics. Twenty percent of the large farmers are Protestants, four times their percentage of the population.

Geographically, the three counties bordering Northern Ireland, Donegal, Cavan, and Monaghan, which were part of the ancient nine-county province of Ulster, contain the largest Protestant population (generally 10-20 percent). Dublin is 9 percent Protestant, and there are tiny enclaves elsewhere. The overwhelming majority of Protestants are members of the once-established Church of Ireland. The Church of Ireland, sometimes called a fox-hunting squirearchy, is part of the Anglican Communion's "low-church" evangelical wing. A few Presbyterians, Methodists, and Jews reside in the Republic. Some of the more prominent examples of Protestant culture include Trinity College in Dublin, the country's premier intellectual center and now relatively secularized; *The Irish Times,* the foremost Irish newspaper and generally a liberal critic of the nation's foibles; and St. Patrick's Cathedral, Dublin, where Jonathan Swift once preached. Nevertheless, there are some real restrictions on Protestant life in Ireland, even though the docile, quiescent Protestant leadership is rarely critical of the set-up. All is not sweetness and light.

Are there any direct examples of discrimination against the Protestant minority? As we shall see, the imposition of Catholic social morality in many spheres of life constitutes an indirect, but real, problem for Protestants. There are occasionally examples of petty harassment, particularly involving mixed marriage problems in rural areas. Some Protestant-owned shops were stoned and burned in the fall of 1972 in County Donegal, and a boycott of Protestants occurred at Fethard-on-Sea because a Catholic changed his faith to

Protestant. A retired British Protestant colonel was mysteriously murdered in County Meath.

In 1956 two Jehovah's Witnesses were assaulted by villagers in Clonlara, County Clare, and had their books and pamphlets publicly burned in the village square on the instigation of the parish priest. The priest and nine of the assailants were sued in the Limerick City Court on July 27 of that year. The District Judge found the defendants guilty but gave them a suspended sentence! In fact, the hapless witnesses were required to keep the peace and fined £200. This decision occasioned a good deal of criticism.

Another similar case which appeared before the Killahoe District Court on September 15, 1958, concerned assaults by several Catholics on three Protestant evangelists. When charges were brought against the perpetrators of the violence, the District Judge ruled in favor of the defendants and dismissed the charges. The Judge declaimed, "When men come into an Irish village and provoke the people by foisting religious views on them, they are abusing whatever rights they have under the Constitution." After this decision, the Protestant Bishop of Limerick questioned whether any citizen could now express views thought unacceptable to the religious majority. Though these cases occurred over a decade ago, they are still recent enough to cause some reflection and concern.

In 1971 in the little village of Fanod, County Donegal, a Church of Ireland rector's study was bombed. The failure of the police to apprehend the culprits disturbed the local Protestants. A Church of Ireland rector of a small church in the Dublin suburbs was abused by vicious phone calls and attacks on his church building. His son was beaten by thugs on his way home from school. The anger was apparently provoked by a mixed-marriage dispute, that poisonous and never-ending problem.

One of the more subtle ways in which Protestants are discriminated against is the requirement that knowledge of Gaelic is essential for civil service employment. Most Protestant schools do not teach Gaelic, so this places them at somewhat of a disadvantage. Even an oral knowledge is required.

Why is the Protestant leadership so docile and undemonstrative? Are they really satisfied with their lot? There is no real explanation for their relative silence. Perhaps they are afraid of stirring up trouble and upsetting the applecart. John Whale, writing in the *London Sunday Times* (January 30, 1972) believes that "Protestants live in a ghetto of the mind" despite relative economic security. "Protestants are on the watch," he says, for "they know, from recurrent signs, that this careful tolerance (in Ireland today) might not last." Conor Cruise O'Brien sarcastically suggests that no matter how badly Protestants might someday be treated, there will always be some Protestant leaders around to tell everyone how well they are treated.

Dr. Noel Browne, a redoubtable anticlerical and one of Ireland's most courageous statesmen, refers to the Protestants as "a tiny unthreatening, decreasing, acquiescent 'Uncle Tom' led minority . . . . " A fascinating letter appeared in the *Irish Times* (Dublin, March 1, 1973) written by a minister who really sums up the problem of Protestant leadership in Ireland. Rev. D.C. Johnston wrote: "While on the perennial subject of mixed marriages, I feel the failure of the Protestant Churches themselves in the Republic to expose the injustices of the Catholic stance over this has not been sufficiently acknowledged.

"For example, Fethard-on-Sea was the last, national test case. Who spoke up, condemning it? The Protestant hierarchy? Not on your life! It was left to two Catholics, Dr. Noel Browne and the Premier, Eamon de Valera, to censure this intolerance. And in other matters of civil rights in the South, it was left to the late Owen Sheehy Skeffington, an agnostic, to do the protesting when human rights were infringed."

Conor Cruise O'Brien reported that "in the harsher climate of 1972, some Protestant congregations in the Republic were warned that the amounts collected from them for the support of families of internees in Northern Ireland would be publicly announced in the locality."

Population statistics are disturbing to many Protestants, who now appear to be a vanishing minority. The serious Protestant decline is revealed in the following data:

(Number of Protestants in Ireland)
1911 — 313,049
1926 — 208,024
1936 — 183,461
1946 — 157,516
1961 — 145,075
1971 — 130,126

Let's look at specific areas of interfaith conflict in Ireland. The "marriage question" is one of the most serious and disturbing and places a cloud over what should be one of life's more joyous experiences. Roman Catholics insist on protecting their religious prerogative in the marital relationship. The issue revolves around the Vatican decree of 1908, "Ne Temere," which demanded written guarantees that any children issuing from a mixed marriage would be raised Catholic. Catholic restrictions on birth control, prohibitions against the Catholic partner's attendance at Protestant services, and the insinuation about converting the non-Catholic were provisions which have poisoned Protestant-Catholic relationships for over a half-century.

The rules were incorporated into the 1917 Code of Canon Law and have been slightly modified in recent years. In 1966, the Vatican Congregation for the Doctrine of The Faith issued a document entitled "Sacrament of Matrimony," which allowed oral rather than written prenuptial guarantees, abolished the Catholic partner's obligation to convert the non-Catholic, and seemed to indicate that dispensations from these rules might be easier to obtain. In 1970 Pope Paul issued a Motu Proprio which declared that in order to obtain a dispensation from the local bishop "the Catholic party shall declare that he is ready to remove dangers of falling away from the faith. He is also gravely bound to make a sincere promise to do all in his power to have the children baptized and brought up in the Catholic faith."

100

Cardinal Conway declared in early 1973 that the antenuptial agreements were no longer really in force in Ireland, a statement welcomed by many Protestant leaders, who see the whole marriage question as central to improving Protestant-Catholic relations. However, many critical comments accused the Cardinal of equivocating. The respected fortnightly *Hibernia* accused the Cardinal of "telling less than the truth when he said that the Protestant partner was not nowadays compelled to make any promises. Surely, the other half of this undoubted truth is that the Catholic partner *is* compelled to make certain promises, and that this—if the Catholic partner is sincere—leaves us with 'Ne Temere' substantially unchanged."

Dr. H.F. Woodhouse, a professor of divinity at Trinity College, branded the Cardinal's statement "disingenuous and misleading." Woodhouse continued, "I can personally produce written statements made in 1972 by Roman Catholic ecclesiastical authorities which prove that the most narrow interpretation is being placed upon clauses of the Motu Proprio." Rev. John Greer, Church of Ireland chaplain to the new University of Ulster in Coleraine, contended the Catholic regulations force the Protestant to violate his conscience and his religious liberty. "It is clear," he said, "that in a mixed marriage, the non-Roman Catholic is denied the right to determine the religious belief of the children."

There have been some encouraging voices from Ireland's famed Roman Catholic seminary, Maynooth, and the Association of Irish Priests, indicating that many younger priests would like to see these marriage laws abolished.

The Catholic Church's immense power in the intermarriage controversy was upheld by the Irish Supreme Court in the 1951 *Tilson* case, a genuine *cause celebre*. In this case, the Supreme Court enforced the prenuptial mixed marriage pledges against a Protestant who married a Catholic and then reneged on the provisions. The Court held that the 1937 Constitution made the mixed-marriage pledge enforceable in civil courts. This intolerable decision indicates some of the difficulties of being a Protestant in Eire. Dr. Kenneth Milne of the Church of Ireland eloquently summarized the Protestant position:

I object to "Ne Temere" not because it affects us numerically but becuase it strikes at the very root of family life. I would go almost so far as to suggest that it is contrary to the spirit, if not the letter, of the basic human rights. It is the great obstacle that exists to the integration of Catholic and Protestant society in Ireland, whatever it may achieve in terms of unconditional surrender.

The consequences of intermarriage are deeply disquieting to the Protestant community. It is the *central factor* in the Protestant decline in Ireland. Since the children of such marriages must be raised as Catholics and since the Protestant birthrate is much lower than the Catholic, it is not surprising that Protestants decline at each succeeding census. The Irish Economic and Social Research Institute estimated that in 1961 one-third of Protestant men and one-fifth of Protestant women married Catholics that year. Protestant church leaders are as opposed to intermarriage under the present conditions as Roman Catholics. The incidence of intermarriage is still quite rare, estimated to be 4 percent or less of all marriages. In addition, adoptions by interfaith couples are forbidden by law. Garret Fitzgerald, the Minister for Foreign Affairs in the new Irish coalition government, and a liberal Catholic, declares in his significant new book *Towards a New Ireland* "The problem posed by the Ne Temere decree on mixed marriages, which has been responsible for a significant part of the decline in the Protestant population of the Republic, is one that can be resolved only by the authorities of the Catholic Church."

Civil divorce is unobtainable in the Republic for Catholics and non-Catholics alike. Article 41, Section 3 states: "41.3.2 No law shall be enacted providing for the grant of a dissolution of marriage." "41.3.3. No person whose marriage has been dissolved under the civil law of any other State but is a subsisting valid marriage under the law for the time being in force within

102

the jurisdiction of the Government and Parliament established by this Constitution shall be capable of contracting a valid marriage within that jurisdiction during the lifetime of the other party to the marriage so dissolved." This imposition of Catholic canon law on civil law was incorporated into the 1937 Constitution. Prior to this, citizens had been given the legal right, under the divorce laws of England, to secure divorce on grounds of adultery. The prohibition of divorce was significantly *not* contained in the 1922 Constitution, because it was seen as an affront to Protestant conscience. The hierarchy, however, marshalled its support and pressured Parliament on the divorce issue. Protestant criticism was mild and respectable, since the tiny minority feared retaliation. William Butler Yeats eloquently protested against this sectarian usurpation declaring, "once you attempt legislation upon religious grounds you open the way for every kind of intolerance and for every kind of religious persecution." Finally in 1973 the Anglican Church of Ireland's 102nd General Synod unanimously urged removal of the constitutional ban on divorce. They said: "Although the various Christian Churches in Ireland are opposed to dissolution of marriage in general, certain exceptions are recognized. In fact, however, the existing provisions have been interpreted as representing the Roman Catholic position and have in that way been religiously divisive . . . "

The prohibition of divorce provisions does not, of course, guarantee marital happiness or stability. It merely insures external conformity and stability. It is possible that those wishing a divorce will go to England or Northern Ireland, though even divorces granted in another country are not recognized in Ireland. Father James Healy, director of the Milltown Institute of Theology and Philosophy in Dublin, reported that marital breakdown is a "serious problem" and cited 2,000 officially registered deserted wives in Ireland. (Religious News Service, February 6, 1973) Rev. Healy and a number of younger priests at Maynooth Seminary are cautiously recommending changes in the Irish law. However, Mr. Lynch's Finance Minister Colley, in 1972, warned against expecting any revision in the divorce laws in the immediate future.

The prohibition against birth control information stems from the Church's fanatical opposition to any family planning information, even in this enlightened age. The Criminal Justice Act of 1935 forbade the sale or importation of contraceptives. The Church insists that artificial contraception frustrates the natural law, and that the state must embody this concept and enforce it in the civil law. This rigidity is laughable and is, I am told, frequently ignored by the young and the well-educated. People frequently purchase contraceptives in Northern Ireland or England. There are rumors of a flourishing contraband contraceptive traffic, though I could not verify these assertions.

This absurd policy naturally disturbs many Protestants and Catholics and the Irish Medical Association, which is becoming increasingly restive under these restrictions. Courageous legislators attempted to amend the ban in 1971 and 1972 but were subjected to intense clericalist pressure. Roman Catholic power can be credited with defeating the birth control reform bill. Dublin's reactionary Archbishop McQuaid warned parliament that repeal of this law would be "gravely damaging to morality" and "a curse upon our country." McQuaid continued:

> Given the proneness of our human nature to evil, given the enticement of bodily satisfaction, given the widespread incitement to unchastity, it must be evident that access to hitherto unlawful contraceptive devices will prove a most certain occasion of sin, especially to immature persons.
>
> The public consequences of immorality that must follow for our whole society are only too clearly seen in other countries.

Then Prime Minister Lynch commented that private morality should not be a subject for legislation. Dr. John O'Connell, editor of the *Irish Medical Times* and a member of Parliament, presented results of a recent poll of Ireland's 2,700 doctors, which showed an overwhelming majority in favor of repeal. After the church's triumph, Dr. Noel Browne castigated the "arrogant authoritarianism of Dr. McQuaid and his comrades."

Roman Catholic hostility to family planning has not abated. In December 1972, Bishop Cornelius Lucey closed the Catholic Marriage Advisory Center in Cork, thereby provoking a public controversy. Dr. Marie O'Sullivan, medical consultant to the center, disclosed that 93 percent of the people using the agency's facilities were seeking advice on family planning. The *Irish Medical Times* denounced the bishop's action as an encroachment on "the right of doctors to publish in good faith medical and scientific facts, without fear or favor."

As this book was going to press in December, Ireland's Supreme Court ruled that the 1935 law against imparting contraceptives was unconstitutional. The case was brought by Mrs. Mary McGee, a fisherman's wife and mother of four children, who claimed that her life would be endangered by more children. A lower court had originally dismissed the case but an appeal was sent to the Supreme Court. The ruling will allow contraceptives to be brought into the country freely, though they may not yet be purchased openly. Parliament must pass enabling legislation for open purchase.

Despite this intransigence, several authorities have noted that a substantial number of Irish girls go to London to give birth to illegitimate children. Of course, this may account for Ireland's low illegitimacy rate compared to England, Scotland, and Northern Ireland.

Ireland's birthrate is not spectacularly high, but this is due to a curious amalgam of late marriages, censorious puritanism, the glorification of celibacy, and emigration of young Irish men and women.

Very little need be said about abortion, since the Roman Catholic Church regards this as a heinous crime and prohibits legal abortions in Ireland, and wherever else the church has sufficient political influence. Despite the church's fanatical opposition to therapeutic abortion, even in a case where a mother's life is in grave jeopardy, it is estimated that 1,000 Irish girls go to England for legal, safe abortions each year.

The Irish Constitution grudgingly acknowledges that education is a government responsibility in most enlightened, modern countries. There is a certain Catholic orientation, especially in the negative way Article 42, Section 3 reads:

1. The State shall not oblige parents in violation of their conscience and lawful preference to send their children to schools established by the State, or to any particular type of school designated by the State.
2. The State shall, however, as guardian of the common good, require in view of actual conditions that the children receive a certain minimum education, moral, intellectual and social.

Section 4 requires the State to give "due regard for the rights of parents, especially in the matter of religious and moral formation."

The Constitution goes on to spell out the relationship between the state and religion in regard to schools. Article 44, Sections 4-6 affirm:

4. Legislation providing State aid for schools shall not discriminate between schools under the management of different religious denominations, nor be such as to affect prejudicially the right of any child to attend a school receiving public money without attending religious instruction at that school.
5. Every religious denomination shall have the right to manage its own affairs, own, acquire and administer property, movable and immovable, and maintain institutions for religious or charitable purposes.
6. The property of any religious denomination or any educational institution shall not be diverted save for necessary works of public utility and on payment of compensation.

Education in Ireland has always been a scandal. Until recent years, education was the stepchild of the Irish budget. Not until 1964 were government grants available for building secondary schools. Thus, for the first time, free secondary education is available to Irish youth. Compulsory school attendance until age 15 became law in 1970.

Ireland has a system of so-called "National Schools" which are, in reality, denominational schools. A new system of vocational-technical schools has been developed and is both nondenominational and expanding. The national schools developed in the nineteenth century when the concept of free, popular education, at least on the primary level, received public acceptance. The churches, both Protestant and Roman Catholic, demanded essential control of the educational process. In 1831 the concept of nondenominational schools was squashed by the hierarchies and a distinctively sectarian orientation was applied to the schools.

The national schools are publicly financed in all respects but the state stands apart from the internal management of the schools. The schools are managed by priests or persons, who, in turn, appoint the teachers. The taxpayers pay all teacher's salaries by public grants, supply the necessary equipment and pay for construction and repair costs. Outside of the vocational schools, 97 percent of the national schools are essentially Catholic, while 3 percent are Protestant. There are even a few Jewish schools in Dublin and Cork, as there are 4,000 Jews in Ireland. The schools are often small, as there are 4,800 primary schools (400 Protestant ones) for 490,000 pupils. Overcrowding in classrooms, however, is a serious problem, as there is an average of 34 pupils per teacher. Incidentally, in some very rural areas, the old one-room school house with a teacher and maybe eight or ten children still exists.

The concept of separation is operative throughout all phases of Irish education, not just in the Protestant-Catholic divisions. The state has almost no direct control of the internal management of the schools. The primary and secondary school systems are distinct, and the vocational schools are a separate entity all together. Rich and poor are separated as are boys and girls in most areas of the country. There are few parent-teacher associations.

107

Though compulsory school attendance has been raised to 15, almost 40 percent of the children receive no further education after primary school. This number is steadily declining, however, since the growth of the vocational school concept. The Ministry of Education is earnestly seeking improvements in all phases of the educational process. Total expenditures on education are rapidly rising, though the Republic still spends less per capita than Northern Ireland or England. Note the increase in educational expenditures by the Irish government:

Fiscal Year	Millions Spent on Education
1968-69	44.6
1969-70	58.3
1970-71	67.6
1971-72	78.8

Historically, only a minority of Irish children were ever able to obtain a secondary school education, since attendance was not compulsory or free. In effect, only the rich or comfortable could attend the secondary schools, which were managed by religious orders, primarily the Christian Brothers. In 1924 the government began to pay the teacher's salaries and to assist with maintenance costs. Since most of the teachers were "religious" rather than lay, the funds went directly to the church coffers. Very few of the teachers had earned university degrees. Today, because of government grants to students, a majority of children now receive secondary education. Secondary school enrollment, for example, increased from 66,000 in 1958 to 118,000 in 1968.

The increasing popularity of vocational schools, which increased in enrollment from 24,000 in 1958 to 42,000 in 1968, is probably due to two factors: the lack of church control and the relevance of the courses to practical realities. The lack of denominational indoctrination may be the secret reason for these schools' support and for the hostility of the hierarchy. The courses prepare the students for specific technical jobs and are appropriate for nonacademically oriented youngsters.

In fact, almost 25 percent of the secondary school children now attend vocational schools. Their growth rate is reflected by the fact that about half of the new students entering school attend the vocationals. In the urban and border districts, these schools are truly interdenominational, but in rural areas they are almost de facto Catholic schools.

In 1971 a major church-state crisis occurred when the Minister for Education made a proposal, without even consulting Protestant authorities, for a post-primary school "rationalization" system that would have involved secondary schools. These so called new "community" schools were to be controlled by the trustees appointed by the local Roman Catholic bishop and managed by committees two-thirds of whose members were to be appointed by the Roman Catholic school authorities. Needless to say, this was viewed as a power-grab by the hierarchy over the last vestige of nondenominationalism in Irish education. This proposal was, in Garret Fitzgerald's words, "indicative of an attitude of mind that can scarcely commend itself to Protestants." Fitzgerald, one of the most perceptive Irish government officials in many a year, continued his analysis, ". . . the fact that his proposal was put forward at a time when there was much public and parliamentary discussion about the need to create in the Republic a pluralistic society of a kind that could be acceptable to Northern Protestants suggests a high degree of insensitivity to this crucial issue at both civil service and ministerial level."

In retrospect, the way in which this dispute was handled probably offended Protestants more than the substance of the proposition. Private consultations between the Department of Education and the Catholic Hierarchy, with Protestant school authorities totally excluded, was rightly seen as an affront to the tiny Protestant community. Furthermore, the vocational schools represented an acceptable education for Protestants in rural areas where no Protestant schools exist.

The government, to its credit, modified and then abandoned these proposals under pressure from a large segment of

the Catholic lay community (especially in the opposition political parties which won the 1973 elections) and the Protestant
churches. This is one of the few defeats the Catholic Hierarchy
has received in contemporary Ireland and it may indicate that
the winds of change are blowing stronger in the Emerald Isle.
The political influence of the clergy is obviously not so great as
it was in the Noel Browne "Mother and Child" affair of 1951.
This defeat also indicates a growing anticlericalism or at least
independence among Catholic politicians.

In the realm of higher education, many significant
changes are occurring. There were 16,000 university students in
Ireland in 1968, and there is a possibility that this figure may be
doubled within a decade. Trinity College, the great bastion of
Anglo-Irish and Protestant culture founded in 1591 by Queen
Elizabeth I, has 3,750 students today, about 1,000 of whom are
Catholics. Nearly half of the students come from Britain and
Northern Ireland. For more than a century until 1970, an official ban on Catholic attendance was imposed by the Archbish-
ops of Dublin. The most recent Archbishop, John McQuaid, a
diehard reactionary, maintained the ban with rhetorical
savagery. However, intellectually talented Catholic students
like Conor Cruise O'Brien and Noel Browne, defied the ban
with impunity. The University College of Dublin, called
"National", is the Catholic university, at least formally.
Observers have noted that there is little distinct denominationalism in either school. The quality of Irish universities is steadily improving though critic Michael Sheehy charges that "the
results of Irish university education are not impressive. Relatively few graduates achieve any real cultural distinction . . ."

One of the most contentious church-state disputes re-
volved around the subject of censorship. A Committee of
Inquiry into Evil Literature, set up in 1926, was symptomatic of
the Jansenistic puritanism which prevails in Ireland. In line
with the vague article of the Constitution, legislation was introduced in 1929 (*Censorship of Publications Act*) which provided
for a Censorship Board under the Ministry for Justice to pass on
the merits of literature. Literature especially singled out for

condemnation were reputedly obscene or pornographic publications, and literature advocating birth control or abortion. The first Censorship Board included a Protestant, three Catholic laymen and a Catholic priest, who served as chairman. The capricious and absurd manner in which the censorship law has been applied rankles Irish intellectuals and has made Ireland the laughing stock of the modern world. From 1930 to 1953, 4,057 books and 376 periodicals were banned by the Censorship Board. Between 1950 and 1955, 3,389 books were banned, an average of 678 per year. Conditions improved somewhat in 1960-65, as only 1,902 books were banned, an average of 380 per year. The number banned dropped to 288 in 1965 and 158 in 1966.

After prohibition by the censors, the customs officers had the authority to seize banned books, "under a 1946 refinement and they were even given the additional authority to apprehend books which, on their inexpert opinion, ought to be banned" writes Donald S. Connery. The 1946 *Censorship of Publications Act* did establish an Appeal Board, which is supposed to take into consideration the artistic or literary merit of a book banned by the Board. However, the book cannot be defended by the publisher or author before the Appeal Board, and the decisions are irrevocable and not subject to judicial review. The battle over banning and "unbanning" books has continued for 25 years and is universally regarded as a farce.

In July 1967 a reform bill was passed by the Dail, providing that books banned before 1955 were "unbanned" and a twelve year limit was to be set on future bannings, except books advocating "artificial contraception or abortion." It is in the latter two categories that Protestants and liberals have their reading rights restricted. It seems almost unbelievable that in this enlightened era, a book delineating the rationale and methodology of family planning cannot be legally published or circulated in the Irish Republic. Even the moderately progressive 1967 act provides that all books can be reexamined and the ban reimposed.

Which books and authors have been hit by this system?

The titles and authors are enumerated in the *Register of Prohibited Publications*. *The Register of Prohibited Publications* lists these categories of material: (1) Books supposedly indecent or obscene. (2) Books which "advocate the unnatural prevention of conception or the procurement of abortion or miscarriage . . . " and (3) Prohibited periodicals.

The differentiation between (1) and (2) is often ludicrous. Dr. Albert Ellis, an eminent humanist-psychiatrist, and Dr. Alan Guttmacher appear in both categories. Dr. Guttmacher's intelligent discussions of marriage and birth control problems are banned. Page after page of books dealing with "marriage", "love" or "sex" are banned. Often, it appears that just having these forbidden words in a book title is sufficient. All of Havelock Ellis' pioneering psychosexual works are proscribed. H.G. Wells *The Work, Wealth and Happiness of Mankind* supposedly violates the Irish conscience. Former American priest Emmet McLoughlin's moving memoir *Peoples' Padre* was condemned in 1955.

Sometimes, even mildly written, delicate interpretations of human sexuality are banned. Dr. Evelyn Mills Duval's *When You Marry*, published by the YMCA's Association Press in 1958 is banned. A slap at Anglicans must be inferred from the banning of Alec Vidler's *Sex, Marriage and Religion*, a moderate Anglican view published in 1941 by the Society for Promoting Christian Knowledge. Vidler is one of England's finest writers in church history and religious subjects.

The following are some of the books banned on the ground that they advocate birth control:

The Art and Science of Love	Dr. Albert Ellis
The Book of Love	Upton Sinclair
Family Limitation	Margaret Sanger
Happiness in Marriage	Margaret Sanger
Having a Baby: A Guide for Expectant Parents	
	Dr. Alan Guttmacher
Love Without Fear	Dr. Eustace Chesser
Marriage and Morals	Bertrand Russell
Morals, Manners and Men	Havelock Ellis

More Essays on Love and Virtue	Havelock Ellis
People's Padre	Emmet McLoughlin
Psychology of Sex	Havelock Ellis
The Second Sex	Simone De Beauvoir
Sex, Marriage and Religion	Alec Vidler
When You Marry	Evelyn Mills Duval
The Work, Wealth and Happiness of Mankind	H.G. Wells

Most of the prohibited books in Part (1) are novels. The majority are mediocre, popular junk, but whether they should be prohibited to mature adults by a government in a democratic society is the real issue. Among the books banned, however, are some highly regarded literary works of the past decade. These include:

1. All of Colin Macinne's "London" novels—Absolute Beginners, Adrift in Soho, City of Spades, etc.
2. An American Dream   Norman Mailer
3. America, With Love   Kathleen Winsor
4. Another County   James Baldwin
5. The Assistant   Bernard Malamud
6. Bonjour Tristesse   Francoise Sagan
7. Boys and Girls Together   William Goldman
8. The Empty Canvas   Alberto Moravia
9. The Exile of Capri   Roger Peyrefitte
10. Gabriela, Clove and Cinnamon   Jorge Amado
11. The Ginger Man   J.P. Donleavy
12. The Group   Mary McCarthy
13. Life at the Top   John Braine
14. A New Life   Bernard Malamud
15. Night Unto Night   Philip Wylie
16. On The Road   Jack Kerouac
17. Our Lady of the Flowers   Jean Genet
18. The Pawnbroker   Edward Lewis Wallant
19. Poor No More   Robert Ruark
20. The Prize   Irving Wallace
21. Run, Rabbit   John Updike
22. A Severed Head   Iris Murdoch
23. The Sin of Father Amaro   Eca de Queiroz

24. A Singular Man   J.P. Donleavy
25. To Feed the Hungry   Danilo Dolci
    Many of the most popular and rather innocuous works of
contemporary fiction are prohibited. For example:
1. Alfie   Bill Naughton
2. The Americanization of Emily   William Bradford Huie
3. Band of Angels   Robert Penn Warren
4. Buddwing (a moving and dramatic account of amnesia)
                                                        Evan Hunter
5. Drive, He Said   Jeremy Larner
6. From the Terrace   John O'Hara
7. Goodbye, Columbus   Philip Roth
8. Here We Go Round the Mulberry Bush   Hunter Davies
9. La Dolce Vita (The Screenplay)   Federico Fellini
10. Some Came Running   James Jones
11. A Summer Place   Sloan Wilson
12. The World of Suzie Wong   Richard Mason
    Light detective fiction often fails to meet the censor's
stringency. Some novels by Belgium's Georges Simenon are
barred.

Leslie Charteris' *The Saint Goes West* and Ian Fleming's
The Spy Who Loved Me are prohibited. (Oddly enough none of
the other dozen or so of Fleming's books are banned, though all
are considered somewhat candid in their treatment of sexual
matters.) How Ernie Kovac's memoir *TV-Medium Rare* could
be banned in any country surpasses my imagination or understanding. Errol Flynn's autobiography *My Wicked, Wicked
Ways* was also banned.

The most incomprehensible of the bannings is Oscar
Lewis' *La Vida,* a brilliant, sensitive, and moving portrayal of
life in rural Mexico.

Henry Spencer Ashbee's critical analysis of the Roman
Catholic Church's *Index of Forbidden Books,* published in
1970, is banned, though it is an impressive work.

Contemporary Spanish novelist Eca de Queiroz' powerful
dramatization of rural Spain, *The Sin of Father Amaro,* is

114

banned. Perhaps this is because it depicts, with realism and honesty, many of the personal failures of the Spanish clergy.

Catholic writers have fared no better than non-Catholic ones. Morris L. West, Muriel Spark, A.J. Cronin, Graham Greene, Frances Parkinson Keyes, Compton MacKenzie, Fulton Oursler, and Henry Morton Robinson have had many of their books banned. Among Irish writers in general, Brendan Behan, St. John Gogarty, James Joyce, Edna O'Brien, Kate O'Brien, Sean O'Casey, Frank O'Connor, Sean O'Faolain, Liam O'Flaherty, Samuel Beckett, and Bernard Shaw have been hard hit.

Other great writers whose works have been execrated by Irish censors include: William Faulkner, Jean-Paul Sartre, John Steinbeck, Ernest Hemingway, Thomas Mann, Sinclair Lewis, Theodore Dreiser, Maxim Gorki, F. Scott Fitzgerald, Aldous Huxley, Arthur Koestler, Andre Malraux, Somerset Maugham, George Orwell, John Dos Passos, Marcel Proust, Budd Schulberg, Dylan Thomas, H.G. Wells, Tennessee Williams, Leo Tolstoy, Voltaire, Sigmund Freud, Emile Zola, Guy de Maupassant, Honore Balzac, C.S. Forester, John O'Hara, Mikhail Sholokov, William Saroyan, J.P. Salinger, Alberto Moravia, Colette, Andre Gide, Saul Bellow, Truman Capote, Norman Mailer, Iris Murdoch, James Michener, Ignazio Silone, J.P. Donleavy, Joyce Cary, C.P. Snow, and Irwin Shaw.

According to most critics the obsession with sex and the tendency to view isolated passages out of context render the whole censorship system absurd. Kate O'Brien's *The Land of Spices,* for example, was banned because of one veiled reference to homosexuality. Books critical of Catholicism, Catholic policy or the Catholic priesthood are often subject to informal pressures. Though not explicitly banned they are rarely purchased for libraries or bookstores lest they offend the superpious.

There are other anomalies in the application of the law. Books such as James Joyce's *Ulysses* and *Finnegan's Wake* were not banned primarily because it was felt they were too complex to be read by the masses anway! Irish censorship law states that the imposition of a ban must be considered in the light of:

1) The language in which it is written
2) The nature and extent of the circulation which it is likely to have
3) The class of reader which may reasonably be expected to buy it

Film censorship, somewhat surprisingly in light of contemporary cinematic candor, is less controversial and a bit less severe. Compared to other European countries, Ireland's is still one of the most strict, if not the strictest. Ever since the 1920s no film has been exhibited in public without a certificate of approval from the film censor. One man exists as film censor and he views over 1,000 films a year.

Film censorship works quietly with no public announcements of bannings other than an annual statistical review. Films are often "cut" and then allowed for exhibition, so many Irish are unaware that they are viewing a truncated film. In 1966, 878 films were passed, 89 were cut and 49 were banned. An Appeal Board often overrules the censor. Some notable films are banned, which angers aesthetically sensitive Irish men and women. Bergman's *The Silence* and Fellini's *La Dolce Vita* were banned; *The Girl With Green Eyes,* based on Edna O'Brien's charming novel *August Is A Wicked Month,* was banned, as was the book. Edna O'Brien seems to be the special *bete noire* of Irish censors, as all five of her sensitive and candid novels of Irish life have been condemned. She is, in fact, Ireland's only talented living novelist but she lives in exile in London because of the "stifling atmosphere" in Ireland.

There is no "official" censorship over the theater, but there is considerable unofficial, indirect, clerical pressure. Some critics believe this priestly censorship has destroyed the creative vitality of the once-famed Abbey Theatre. As recently as 1957, Tennessee Williams' *Rose Tattoo* was closed by police.

In 1958, church pressure led to the withdrawal of a new Sean O'Casey play and a proposed dramatization of *Ulysses*. In all fairness, it is unlikely that this would happen today.

A certain brand of unofficial censorship still exists in parts of Ireland. Even though the Vatican has abolished the *Index of Prohibited Books*, Ireland, being more Catholic than Rome, has not implemented the liberalization. Most of the works on the *Index* have been quietly and effectively excluded from Irish bookshops and libraries. One can search in vain for Zola, Anatole France, Voltaire, Kant, Gide, Sartre, Bergson, Gibbon, Paine, Balzac, Hugo and many other literary luminaries in Irish public libraries.

Despite the censorship hassle, intelligent well-read people can bring back as much "proscribed" literature from London or Belfast as they wish. These restrictions, though rancorous, are often bypassed and shown to be ludicrous. Ireland would do well to abolish its censorship statutes and enter the modern world. At the very least, Irish parliamentarians should be given a copy of Milton's *Areopagitica* (if it isn't banned). Arland Ussher concluded in his *The Face and Mind of Ireland* that "censorship is maintained primarily for the purpose of baiting the intellectuals."

Is there any substantial trend toward anticlericalism in Ireland today? Does everyone quaver when the hierarchy speaks? Many observers, including many Catholic ones, have noted an increasing disinclination to accept clerical direction of society. Criticism of the Church's social and educational policies appears with frequency these days.

Anticlericalism has always been a part of Irish life, especially among young intellectuals. It could be argued that even the great Daniel O'Connell, who stated that he took his religion from Rome but his politics from home, was somewhat anticlerical. Michael McCarthy, author of the classics *Priests and People in Ireland* and *Rome in Ireland* around the turn of this century, was one of the most militant anticlericals ever to write in the English language. He severely condemned the Church as the great barrier to progress and culture in his beloved Ireland.

Most of Ireland's great writers from Joyce to Shaw were critical of the Church's role in Irish culture, while recognizing that an amalgam of historical factors made the Catholic clergy the best educated and most influential members of society. As lay education increased steadily through the 20th century, this is no longer true. Historically, in Catholic lands, increasing popular education and enlightenment inevitably lead to a diminution of the Church's political and cultural power.

A contemporary anticlerical Michael Sheehy writes: "Irish Catholicism stands censured, or condemned, by the majority of intellectually distinguished Irishmen." He further declares "The Irish Catholic clergy oppose vital human growth of every sort; discourage thought and art; stifle criticism; try to keep the public like an obedient flock of sheep. As a result, Irish Catholicism has no distinctive social, intellectual and artistic character." Until his death a few years ago, Sen. Owen Sheehy Skeffington of Trinity College valiantly opposed clericalism.

Today's leading critic of Catholic power is Dr. Noel C. Browne, a member of the Irish Dail for over 20 years and now a member of the prestigious Irish Senate. Browne, writing in the American monthly *Church & State* (February 1973) charges that the church "predetermines the social and economic policies of our society by her control of our primary educational system." Browne believes that certain subjects are sacrosanct and taboo, and cannot be changed by the legislature or the judiciary because of the unwritten, indirect control of the Catholic Church. "She insists," he says "on our acceptance of a clear, ideological position on all social and economic matters." Browne also believes that the Constitution's Article 44 "has been used in our courts to give to Catholic canon law the authority of our civil law, and used in Parliament to justify the imposition of Catholic social teaching in our laws."

Dr. Browne angrily concludes "While there are other Catholic European states, there are none outside Spain and

118

Portugal in which the church is as powerful politically and spiritually corrupted by wealth and position as is the Irish Catholic Church."

As we can see from reading Dr. Browne, criticism of clericalism is fairly widespread and respectable, especially among intellectuals, in Ireland. The tone of anticlericalism is not as virulent as in many Latin countries. Donald Connery comments "Anticlericalism is rife in Ireland, but it has no element of anti-Christianity. Rather, it is fault-finding on a grand scale by Catholics frustrated by the conservatism of the Church or resentful of the high-handedness of individual priests and of their own sheeplike status."

In closing, a few statistics on the extent of Catholicism in Ireland are in order. For approximately three million Catholics, there are 6,000 priests, 13,000 nuns, and 2,000 Christian Brothers. In addition, Ireland imports more priests for missionary endeavors than any other country in the world. There are 6,672 Irish priests in seventy overseas lands. Recent sociological surveys indicate that 90 to 95 percent of Catholics attend weekly mass, surely the highest church attendance rate in the world. The percentage approaches 100 in rural areas and even three-fourths of University students practice their faith regularly.

As this book was going to press in December 1973, a sociological survey released in Dublin revealed that only 47% of Dublin Catholics now attend Sunday mass regularly and that one-third of university students are "permanently estranged" from their faith. Though Dublin may not be representative of Ireland as a whole, this is a startling and dramatic evidence of Catholic decline even in this most Catholic land.

HEAVEN SHALL SMILE ON ULSTER YET

Heaven shall smile on Ulster yet
Though trembling hearts despair.
The pain, the tumult, and the grief
Are upward borne in prayer.
The saints beleagured, and forlorne
Seek out the God of Grace —
For Ulster in the Sovereign Will
Retains that destined place.

Think on King William and the Boyne
On Cooke and Hanna too —
The Grace of God has touched this shore
And brought us safely through.
Heroes enfamed in days of yore
All speak with staunch accord
Of Ulster's stand 'gainst Harlot Rome
In triumph for the Lord.

Rome rages still with mighty power
Against this favoured place
Dare we dispute and put our trust
In other than God's Grace.
The sword of Gideon and the Lord
Shall ever be our cry
In Orange fervour, Faith and fight
Let all our ensigns fly.
For Heaven shall smile on Ulster yet
And Protestants in praise
Shall see God's mighty arm made bare
Just as in former days.

A.C.S.

7. Candles in the Dark

In April 1973 I undertook, on behalf of *Church & State,* a journey to England and Northern Ireland to see for myself what is happening to interfaith relationships in that tumultous divided province.

I suppose the most immediate recollection is the feeling of being in a war zone when one arrives in Belfast, after stringent security procedures at London Airport. One sees heavily armed British soldiers throughout the airport and on the road to Belfast. Tanks and landrovers patrol the streets of Belfast, and, indeed, the villages and towns of this embattled province.

Another distinct aspect which stands out in my memory are the outward manifestations of official Christianity. There are 265 churches in Belfast, or one for every 1,500 people. Over 98 percent of the people are enrolled members of some church. Church attendance runs higher than almost any major city in the world, excluding perhaps Dublin. Signs abound everywhere exhorting the faithful: "God is the answer to Ulster's problem," "One way," "True Peace is Jesus," "The End is Near," "Jesus is Coming," "Flee From the Wrath to Come," "Get Right with God," etc. (If one strays into the Shankill, he will see the intense lack of admiration for the Pope expressed vividly!) On the Antrim Road alone, one can visit a Christian bookstore, Evangelical bookstore, and Presbyterian bookstore. All of this might appear impressive to the casual observer until one remembers the horrible tragedies and atrocities that have been committed in the last four years, at least partially in the name of God or "religion." One gentleman farmer from County Tyrone told me he wishes the churches could be abolished in Ireland and then a little Christianity (could be) introduced!

Northern Ireland, despite its present troubles, is an impressively beautiful land. The sandy beaches, the Marne Mountains, Cave Hill, the charming villages and rolling farmland, and the Giant's Causeway are among Europe's scenic treasures. Belfast is another story, an industrial city that has burgeoned in less than a century. It is stodgy, pragmatic, sober. Even within Belfast contrasts occur. In riot and bomb scarred West Belfast, where working-class Protestants and Catholics live in grim proximity, a perceptible but indefinable sense of fear and tension pervades the air. However, the beautiful area around Queens University in South Belfast appears untouched by the "troubles."

I was advised in London to be very cautious in Belfast and not to take any taxis at the airport under any circumstances. Taxis, I was told, are as sectarian as everything else in this divided society and one might be taken to the wrong district and never seen again. So I took the airline bus, which meets each overseas flight, to the Great Victoria Street railway station, a few yards from the well-guarded Europa Hotel. The bus goes through the Shankill, the center of militant Protestants and the Ulster Defence Association (the Protestant equivalent of the Irish Republican Army.) Prominently displayed are the Union Jack and the Ulster "red hand" flag. Between the Shankill and the center of Belfast there is much evidence of destruction.

Later, driving along a country road with a friend, a Belfast industrialist, we were stopped by British security forces and our car was inspected for bombs. The soldiers were friendly and courteous, but the incident helped one understand the tension and fear that people in Ulster must live with daily. I went into several book stores in Belfast for research materials and in two of them had to ring the bell on the outside of the building and identify myself before being admitted. One major bookseller now sells books from his home because his other locations have been bombed. He told me that on my next trip to Belfast I should phone him from the airport and have one of his staff deliver me safely to his home, where I could stay overnight and do my book browsing. He also told me of the almost total collapse of social life in Belfast since 1969. It is not surprising that Belfast has lost 50,000 people in the last five years, most of them to pleasant suburbs and such new towns as Craigavon.

Many people in recent years have applied to emigrate to Canada, Australia, and New Zealand. Significantly, there is no movement to the Republic of Ireland or to the United States. Emigration has always been a stabilizing factor in Irish history for both North and South. Roman Catholics have a 40 percent higher birthrate than Protestants, but the Catholic emigration rate has always been significantly higher. In each census from 1911 to 1961, the Catholic percentage of the Northern Ireland population remained about 35 percent. There has not been a recent religious census, but the Catholic population has probably increased only slightly above that figure.

The magnitude of the Ulster conflict becomes apparent when one realizes that if the United States had been embroiled in comparable internal strife over 130,000 Americans would be dead and 1,560,000 would be injured. As of this writing, 890 people have died and 10,000 have been injured in Ulster since 1969 in a land whose population approximates that of greater Atlanta.

The last two years have seen an increasing polarization between the religious communities. Random assassinations cost the lives of 81 Catholics and 40 Protestants in 1972 alone. Thousands of families living in mixed neighborhoods, generally members of the minority faith in the area, have been intimidated into relocating to sectarian ghettoes. School vandalism and truancy have increased markedly. Assaults on church and church property have caused considerable disruption of church life. Catholic workers have been harassed in the Harland and Wolff Shipyards, employing 10,000 workmen, leaving very few Catholic employees. Many Catholics have refused to pay rents and rates since August 1971, when internment was introduced, a costly action resented by many Protestants.

How do Ulster residents see the situation today? Four typical individuals presented vastly divergent views. A Belfast industrialist, a Protestant, blamed much of the Ulster troubles on the "welfare ethic," on the world-wide romanticizing of revolution, and on media sensationalism. He insisted that good interfaith relations prevailed in his office and neighborhood.

The Rev. Martin Smyth, a prominent Orange Order chaplain and Presbyterian pastor, accused the international media of distorting Ulster's conflict and maligning the Protestant sector. He also believed there was a cycle of world-wide rebelliousness which accentuated religious and cultural divisions. Smyth was critical of recent Stormont regimes and the British government for allegedly failing to maintain law and order. He asserted that the police had been unjustly condemned and that internment should have been introduced earlier and with more severity. Though a staunch loyalist, Smyth implied that Ulster may have to go it alone and declare independence if the British resolve wavers.

A factory worker, an IRA supporter, blamed the British government for oppressing the common people and forcing an unnatural partition of the island. Though supporting a united Ireland, he believes in a "federal" system where Ulster would retain its "autonomy" within a new Irish state. He asserted that Ulster was "Ireland's greatest province" and that a united Ireland would greatly benefit from its industry and progressive spirit. He criticized the Roman Catholic hierarchy for allegedly supporting the establishment and the British government at critical junctures in Irish history. He and a pro-IRA priest I met both criticized their church leadership harshly and endorsed church-state separation as a desirable objective for their country!

124

A young woman in her 20s from Lurgan said that she, as a Catholic, had felt inferior all of her life and believed that certain job opportunities were closed to her because of her religion. She felt her education had not prepared her for a decent job and stated a preference for mixed schooling. She had no Protestant friends until she moved to London, where she now lives, and now has a Protestant girl friend. She was critical of politicians on both sides and hoped that the troops would leave soon.

A highlight of my trip to Northern Ireland was an interview with former Prime Minister (1963-69) Terence O'Neill, now Lord O'Neill of the Maine.

Lord O'Neill believes that the recent British White Paper is generally constructive but that it alone cannot guarantee peace. He cautioned that the new system of proportional representation may increase the extremist contingent, though it is worth a risk to try the new system.

Lord O'Neill believes that the new coalition government in Dublin may contribute to a resolution of the Ulster problem if it pursues a tougher policy toward the IRA. He warned, however, against unrealistic expectations since the two previous coalition governments in the Republic pursued negative policies toward the North.

"The churches," he added, "have lost all influence because they showed no courage in the early stages of this problem. With a few honorable exceptions, church leaders were too timid and frightened to support moves toward peace and harmony." O'Neill also suggested that de facto religious segregation in education is a fundamental problem because it discourages friendship and perpetuates divisions.

The only hopeful forecast, he concluded, was that "an unwilling peace may be brought about by mutual exhaustion."

Are there no rays of interfaith sunshine in Ulster today? Do all despair? On the contrary, I encountered some genuine rays of sunshine breaking through the long dark night of despair.

There are a number of courageous organizations and individuals working for Protestant-Catholic amity. It is their story that needs telling if Americans and other outsiders are to form a balanced perspective of Northern Irish life.

The Corrymeela Fellowship is a positive force for good as it attempts to bring Catholic and Protestant children together for socially productive endeavors. It has an unobtrusive headquarters in central Belfast and works quietly for peace and understanding. The Fellowship, under the direction of Rev. Ray Davey, also maintains a seaside resort hostel at Ballycastle, a lovely town on the North Antrim coast 50 miles north of Belfast.

The resort center, which has four full-time staff members, stands on seven acres of land overlooking the coastline. Over 6,000 people visited the center last year. It is an oasis in a troubled land. Rev. Davey states, "Corrymeela is essentially a community of Christian people from all the main denominations, who are committed to the work of reconciliation in a divided land." Each summer around 250 young volunteers come to work camps, as well as Christmas and Easter conferences. One of these conferences, known as Corrymeet, discussed the implications of "The Christian Faith Today" and was attended by 80 young people, 18-30 years of age.

Corrymeela concentrates on productive projects in some of Belfast's most troubled areas. The group meets weekly in Belfast and spends one weekend a month at the holiday camp. They rely primarily on voluntary contributions and student workers. The group is kept purposely small so that the young people, generally from Belfast's tough "tribal" slums can develop meaningful and lasting friendships. Small "minibuses" transport the participants back to their respective ghettos. There are approximately 30 young people participating in the project now. There are serious risks involved for the youngsters because of suspicion which exists in their own communities. It is a courageous effort, requiring diligence and patience on the part of the workers and young people.

126

Another man who exhibits heroic courage and magnanimity of spirit is Rev. Joseph Parker, a Church of Ireland minister to seamen. After the tragic death of his son in the carnage of "Bloody Friday" in 1972, Rev. Parker founded his own "Witness for Peace." His signs urging people to "be just and generous" blanket downtown Belfast. While so many others who have also lost loved ones have turned to bitterness and hatred, Rev. Parker shows in his own life the redemptive power of forgiveness.

Protestants and Catholics organized a prayer service for peace last October and 5,000 people spontaneously gathered in the city cemetery. Roman Catholic churches throughout Ireland organized a triduum (3-day period) of prayer for peace during Lent, 1973. At the same time, Protestants and Catholics jointly distributed St. Luke's Gospel in a special edition titled "Good News for Ireland" in modern English.

An organization working for peace in the grim city of Londonderry, is Forderry House, affiliated with the Fellowship of Reconciliation. This group tries to build up trust and respect between the Protestant and Catholic communities. They conducted a 24-hour vigil for peace last Christmas and have encouraged improved housing for the poor of both faiths.

Two events occurring spontaneously indicate the possible thawing of Protestant-Catholic tensions. Two Roman Catholic churches in Upper Falls Road, Corpus Christi and St. John's arranged a Palm Sunday visit to the city cemetery for many Protestant families who have been afraid to visit the graves of loved ones because of the violence since 1971. A similar gathering occurred in December 1972, attended by over 500 people. Roman Catholic parishioners supplied cars and minibuses to the Protestants and were present at the cemetery to greet the visitors.

Canon Patrick Murphy wrote in his parish newsletter:

In these days of confusion and division in the community we welcome the opportunity of making this gesture to

127

our fellow citizens. We pray God that it may be successful as before and that it will continue to imprrove understanding and reconciliation.

(*Belfast Telegraph*, April 13, 1973)

Recently Right Reverend George Quinn, the Church of Ireland's Bishop of Down and Dromore, appealed for funds to help rebuild St. Anthony's Roman Catholic chapel, which was damaged by hooligan terrorists. This is another act of charity and compassion which might not have occurred two or three years ago.

There are two additional organizations worth mentioning. One is PACE (Protestant and Catholic Encounter), an interdenominational peace group rather closely associated with the New Ulster Movement. They recently proposed that local defense corps be set up, under the supervision of the security forces, to combat intimidation in housing areas.

The honorary general secretary of PACE, Rev. Desmond Mock, urged that Protestants and Catholics stand together against the terrible scourge of intimidation, which has driven thousands from their homes in Ulster since 1969. A recent report revealed that 60,000 people have been forcibly relocated in Ulster since 1969, the highest displacement of people in Europe since the Second World War.

PACE urged the authorities to cease using the terms "Protestant" and "Catholic" to classify each murder victim or destroyed property. "There seems to be a scorecard being kept, which encourages revenge," said Mr. Mock.

PACE's director had some appropriate words for the politicians:

They bear a grave responsibility; every death is the result of their past lack of good sense. They should all have been concentrating on building a harmonious community instead of continually highlighting and amplifying differences, thus inflaming people to the extent where they had so lost reason as to allow terrorists to claim to act on their behalf.

(*Irish Times*, Dublin, March 1, 1973)

128

"Women Together," founded in September 1970, has become a source of harmony and hope in the troubled cities of Ulster. It has started a credit union, reopened a youth club, arranged children's outings and dinners for the elderly, developed playgrounds, replaced burnt-out street lights, and helped the cleanup and repair operations after serious riots. Mrs. Monica Patterson, an English-born Roman Catholic, is chairman and chief organizer of the group, which includes women of both faiths. Mrs. Patterson came to the United States in the fall of 1972 for a three-week speaking engagement, impressing audiences everywhere with her courage and sincerity. She spoke at Washington National Cathedral on October 22 and succinctly stated: "It isn't enough to pray for peace. You must pray and *work* for peace."

It is difficult to know what ultimate influence these events will have, but it is encouraging to know that some people in this strife-torn land are willing to light candles rather than to curse the darkness.

ULSTER'S CALL
TO ARMS

**A poem produced in 1939
at the outbreak of war**

Attend you gallant Ulstermen
    Of every degree,
And take your stand to hold
    your land
    For Faith and Liberty.
One Cause, One Heritage,
    One Crown,
Let Ulster's deeds of high
    renown
    Resolve you to be free.

Let canting cranks partition
    prate,
    Oppression falsely cry,
Religious grievances create,
    You know the oft-told lie.
No matter what the fresh dis-
    guise
You are the chosen sacrifice,
    Stand to your arms—or die.

Your fathers fought and toiled
    of old
    An empire to create ;
Yourselves have formed and
    sworn to hold
    Ulster an Empire State.

Then send the message clear
    and plain :
    'Ulster with Britain will re-
    main'.
The foe is at the gate,
    Issue the challenge bold
    and stern :
To all whom it may concern
    Ulster will keep the Gate.

8.   American Aid

Americans of many religious and ethnic groups have often taken strong positions on the treatment of coreligionists abroad. The concern of American Jews over the plight of Soviet Jewry today is evidence. Strong pressure has been placed on the United States government to intercede with the Soviet government to allow Jews to migrate to Israel. In the late 1950s and early 1960s many American Protestants expressed concern to the State Department over the persecution of Protestants in Colombia and Spain. President Eisenhower was encouraged by Protestants to seek better treatment of Protestants in Spain during the President's visit to Franco in 1959. Presidents Theodore Roosevelt and Wilham Howard Taft were praised by American Jews in the early 1900s after they protested against pogroms in Czarist Russia and Rumania. It is no surprise, then, that many Irish-American Catholics would express concern over the Ulster situation.

There has been some influence of Irish-Americans on U.S. policy. In 1888 Irish-American political pressure forced President Cleveland to expel the British ambassador, Sir Lionel Sackville-West after he had publicly expressed confidence that British interests would be safe while Cleveland was in office. In 1912 bitter Irish-American opposition helped defeat the Anglo-American Arbitration Treaty. In 1915 Irish (and German) Americans rallied against the possible admittance of the

131

United States into World War I. Shortly after the war 134 members of the U.S. House of Representatives cabled Prime Minister Lloyd George, urging him to "free" Ireland. Irish-Americans lent strong financial and moral support to the struggle for Irish independence in 1918-23. When civil rights agitation by Ulster Catholics began in 1968, a number of committees and organizations were formed among Irish-Americans to support the Catholic cause and Irish unification.

The U.S. Census for 1970 listed 13,282,000 Americans (6.7 percent of the total population) of Irish ancestry. It is generally assumed, based on most available evidence, that the vast majority are Catholic. The Irish Catholic vote is estimated at 7-8 percent of the total electorate. The Irish Protestant vote is negligible.

Bernadette Devlin visited the United States in 1969 and again in 1971 for a series of well-publicized speeches and fund-raising events. Though some enthusiasm was expressed for her, it is generally conceded that her escapades were unsuccessful. She apparently raised only a fraction of the desired funds. Her close identification with Marxism and revolution, her attacks on the police (largely Irish-American in such major cities as New York, Boston and Chicago) and support for the Black Panthers turned off the basically conservative Irish-American community. Some support was achieved, however. The *New York Daily News* (August 17, 1969) reported that "Irish-American organizations in New York, Chicago and Philadelphia have sent men, weapons and money to Northern Ireland to help rioters battling British troops and the Ulster constabulary. For the last two days, small volunteer groups, carrying money, weapons and ammunition, have been slipping out of Kennedy Airport bound for Dublin and Shannon." A number of ad hoc groups, the United Ireland Committee, the American-Irish Action Committee and the American Congress for Irish Freedom, raised thousands for "bullets and bandages." The opposition to so-called British imperialism was the main impetus for the groups. Religion was rarely mentioned. Joseph O'Connor of the United Ireland Publicity Committee candidly admitted: "We have been waiting for this a long time. We are using every method possible to wage a full-scale civil war in the six northern counties."

The *Belfast News Letter* (April 13, 1973) reported that several hundred thousand dollars a year were donated in the United States to the Irish Northern Aid Committee, reliably reported to be the main front for the Provisional IRA. America is also the direct source for much IRA weaponry and war material. The *Manchester Guardian* in February 1972 claimed that sixty chapters of this group in the USA had sent $250,000 to the Provos. These committees have no control over the spending of the funds raised.

Apparently the British government has persuaded the U.S. authorities to crack down on the Provo front groups. In June 1972 five Irish-Americans from New York were arrested in Fort Worth, Texas for refusing to answer grand jury questions about alleged gunrunning to Ulster. They were incarcerated in the federal prison at Seagoville, Texas. On July 5, 1973 U.S. District Judge Leo Brewster denied appeals from the men and said they must remain in prison until the present term of the grand jury expires in November. Needless to say, this has inflamed pro-IRA opinion in America. A "Dallas Defense Fund Committee" has been established by the Irish Institute in New York. The National Association for Irish Freedom has taken up the cudgels and charged on July 6, 1973 that the governments of Britain, the Irish Republic and the United States have conspired against the "Fort Worth Five."

One of the strongest supporters of the Fort Worth Five is the Roman Catholic Bishop of Corpus Christi, Texas the Most Reverend Dr. Thomas J. Drury. Bishop Drury, a native of Ireland, denounced the imprisonment as "a complete travesty on justice." Dr. Drury wrote to President Nixon that the five were unjustly imprisoned 1,400 miles from home and family. The *Irish Advocate* (July 7, 1973), an Irish-American weekly newspaper published in New York since 1893, reported that the

133

bishop drives to see the prisoners every week and charged that "Texas is prejudiced against these men." Bishop Drury frequently addressed rallies on their behalf.

Father William Cunningham, a Jesuit law dean, and lawyer for the five, charged that the case may have been linked to the Watergate scandal. He told Judge Brewster that former White House assistant John Caulfield, a Watergate-linked flunkie, had "earned an award for turning in a group of Irish radicals in the Bronx." The case was finally resolved on August 13, 1973 when the five were released by a federal judge following an order from U.S. Supreme Court Justice William O. Douglas to free the men. No further investigation into the alleged smuggling is anticipated.

An extreme leftwing group, "Youth Against War and Fascism" has fomented demonstrations in several U.S. cities. It is somewhat surprising that the international Left has rallied to the Catholic cause in Ulster. No so many years ago the Catholic Church was regarded as a medieval, reactionary obstruction to the new social and political order being planned by the Left. It is possible that this apparent shift in policy is due to the accommodation being reached by the Vatican with various Communist governments. Perhaps the Vatican regards Communism as the wave of the future and wants to secure some rights of existence in case Communism becomes the dominant political force of the 21st century.

The Irish Northern Aid Committee, with headquarters in the Bronx, New York, has been required since April, 1970 to register with the Internal Security Section, Criminal Division of the U.S. Department of Justice. This requirement is based on the *Foreign Agents Registration Act of 1938* as amended.

I went to the Justice Department's files on this group and discovered that a considerable amount of funds have been raised among sympathetic Irish-Americans and sent to the Northern Aid Committee in Belfast by courier. The group did not release reports of official remittances to Ulster until January 30, 1972. It is now required to submit biannual financial reports to the Justice Department. For the period August 1,

134

1971 to January 30, 1972 the Committee sent $128,099 to Belfast. Funds were sent to Mr. Joseph Cahill, a notorious IRA fugitive, and to Mr. Joseph Clarke.

The following is a summary of funds sent to Belfast by this Committee.

	Amount
August 1, 1972 to January 29, 1973	$150,437.97
February 1, 1972 to July 29, 1972	$312,700.00
August 1, 1971 to January 30, 1972	$128,099.00
Total	$591,236.97

The above figures are, of course, volunteered by the Committee itself. It could very well be a conservative figure. Funds collected before August 1, 1971 have never been reported.

Occasionally, bank drafts are sent to Belfast but more often large sums of cash ($20,000 to $40,000) are carried by messenger directly to the strife-torn province. It is interesting that the August 1972 to January 1973 report indicated that $44,700 was "ear-marked for defendants relief only and were cleared through the Prisoners' Dependents Relief Fund." The other $105,737 was sent by courier to Belfast. Where did it go? To buy guns and bombs to bring more sorrow and misery to the innocent long-suffering citizens of Ulster? Even the so-called Prisoners' Dependents Relief Fund is a sham, because the families and dependents of the internees have continued to receive generous social welfare benefits from the Ulster government, some for as long as two years!

The NAC listed collections for the six-month period ending January 29, 1973, as "approximately $172,000." The Committee has also spent funds in the U.S. on various propaganda activities. The following is a summary:

	Disbursements
August 1, 1972 to January 31, 1973	$41,388.48
February 1, 1972 to July 29, 1972	25,440.07
August 1, 1971 to January 29, 1972	12,738.84
February 1, 1971 to July 29, 1971	16,075.00
Total	$95,642.39

135

What have the disbursements gone for? There are no full-time staff members. All are part-time volunteers. The three directors of the NAC are retired Irish-Americans from the Queens borough of New York. All three are naturalized American citizens. The group lists expenditures for radio programs, newsletters, printing and advertising, legal fees, travel, rent, merchandising, publicity, book sales and the dissemination of political propaganda. Documents filed by the Committee with the Justice Department claim that the Committee seeks "to counteract British propaganda and to channel funds and clothing to the refugees in Ulster." They "publicize the conditions in the six counties" and "aid the suffering victims of oppression and religious persecution."

A curious figure surfaced in the United States in the fall of 1972. He is Father Sean McManus, a priest deeply involved in IRA activities, and the brother of Frank McManus, the member of Parliament for the Westminster constituency of Fermanagh and South Tyrone. McManus is in semi-exile from Ulster and now functioning in the Baltimore Archdiocese. He has quickly resumed his political agitation activities, having established chapters of the NAC at the Cathedral of Mary Our Queen in Baltimore and other Catholic parishes in the area. (See the Baltimore *Catholic Review,* February and March 1973 issues.)

The National Association for Irish Freedom, headquartered in New York City, was founded in 1971 and is the main support group in the United States for the Northern Ireland Civil Rights Association. Its sponsors include some prominent Americans, such as Reverend Ralph Abernathy, who seeks to apply the principles of the black civil rights movement in America to the civil rights struggle in Northern Ireland; Congressman Philip Burton, a liberal Democrat of California; Episcopal Bishop C. Kilmer Myers of the Diocese of New York; a prominent New York attorney, Paul O'Dwyer; and it also includes journalist Pete Hamill and a number of individuals from the entertainment world: Richard Conte, Elliott

136

Gould, Arlo Guthrie, Dick Gregory, Pete Seeger, Mary Travers, Dalton Trumbo, Robert Wagner, Gene Kelly and Richard Harris.

The Preamble to the Association states:

"The purpose of the National Association for Irish Freedom is to establish broad public support in the United States for the Northern Ireland Civil Rights Association and to assist the Irish people in their struggle for self-determination. The NAIF supports the right of all people to a standard of living which allows them to live with dignity and supports the right of every nation to self-determination and is opposed to any form of economic, political or military imperialism. The NAIF is opposed to all forms of racism, chauvinism and religious bigotry."

"The NAIF is the coordinating body dedicated to enlisting aid from the American people for civil rights and political freedom in the 32 counties in Ireland." Hence the aim of this group is the support of progressive change-oriented forces in both the North and South of Ireland. The group lists four aims:

1. The primary emphasis of the National Association for Irish Freedom is on the achievement of full civil rights in Northern Ireland through the Northern Ireland Civil Rights Association.
2. To educate the American public on conditions in Ireland and on the issues involved in the present struggle for justice.
3. To assist in the organization of groups throughout the United States to support the Irish struggle for civil rights and political freedom.
4. To protect the rights of Irish and Irish-Americans in this country through non-violent action.

This organization claims to be a "democratic non-violent and non-sectarian organization." It works in many areas, and particularly seeks to counter what it regards as incorrect media presentation of the Ulster struggle. They raise funds to transmit to the Northern Ireland Civil Rights Association. Representatives of NAIF have appeared on radio and television programs

137

in the United States, testified before the House Subcommittee on Foreign Affairs in Washington in 1972, and presented testimony before the Republican Party's subcommittee on Foreign Affairs which drafted the 1972 Republican platform.

In a nutshell NAIF favors support for the Civil Rights movement in Northern Ireland, which includes the withdrawal of British troops, the release of all internees, the abolition of the Special Powers Act, an end to anti-Catholic discrimination in Ulster, and a new political system for Northern Ireland.

In regard to American policy NAIF claims that the Nixon Administration gave permission for Britain to cut 4,000 troops from its NATO commitment in Germany in order to send these troops to Northern Ireland. It has denounced this policy and also claims that the Nixon Administration unlawfully arrested the "Fort Worth Five."

The NAIF publishes a monthly journal *Irish Freedom News*, maintains a number of chapters around the country and published a book entitled *Massacre at Derry* which purports to be the true story of the alleged British massacre of 13 unarmed civil right demonstrators on January 30, 1972 in Londonderry.

The NAIF and the NICRA have also criticized the government of the Irish Republic, for allegedly maintaining a repressive anti-Democratic regime. "The NAIF in its work for Irish freedom, sees and acknowledges the fact that many changes will have to be made in the South of Ireland before unification becomes a reality. It has been made quite clear to the rest of the world that repression in the Republic of Ireland is widespread." It goes on to maintain that there is very little difference between the regimes of North and South Ireland. The NICRA would like to see a more liberal regime in both parts of Ireland. The NAIF criticizes the Irish Republic in the following words. "Ireland has an approximate per capita income of $1400, an 11 percent rate of inflation, 7 percent rate of unemployment, the lowest gross national product of the Common Market nations and 80 percent of the wealth is controlled by 10 percent of the population."

138

NAIF developed a coalition known as the Irish American Coalition to protest the visit of Ireland's former Prime Minister Jack Lynch in January 1973. These organizations include the following: the American Committee for Ulster Justice, the New York Chapter of the Ancient Order of Hibernians, the Anti-Internment Coalition, the Gaelic Athletic Association, the Irish Institute, the Irish Northern Aid Committee, the Irish Republican Clubs of the United States and Canada, the National Association of Irish Freedom, and the Irish Counties Association. A spokesman for the groups has estimated that 50,000 New Yorkers belong to these organizations, though that may be an inflated figure.

In the fall of 1972 NAIF polled the New York congressional delegation to see if they were sympathetic to the civil rights movement in Ulster and opposed to the use of American NATO troops in connection with Ireland. The following Congressmen supported NAIF's position: Bella Abzug, Joseph Addabo, Jonathan Bingham, James J. Delaney, Edward Koch and Joseph J. Minish. All are Democrats. Congressmen Lent, Badillo and Celler indicated general support, as did Liz Holtzman who defeated Congressman Celler.

The group has attacked the American news coverage of Ulster, claiming that it overemphasizes the religious aspects of the crisis and unduly supports British policy. The *Irish Freedom News,* October 1972, claims "the news media in the United States has managed to distort the situation in Northern Ireland so that Americans are unable to grasp the totalitarian nature of the British rule in Northern Ireland. The liberal and conservative press alike present a picture of a benign British government trying to bring peace to the mad bloody Irish."

The group is genuinely nonsectarian and has support from many religious groups. Rev. Ted Veekler, pastor of the Flatbush Presbyterian Church in Brooklyn, supports the group and says "the Northern Ireland Civil Rights Association has denounced the preaching and teaching of fear and hatred based on religious identification."

139

How much support does the NAIF have among Irish Americans? It is probably very limited because most Irish Americans have elected to stay out of the trouble in Northern Ireland. For example, NICRA organizer Kevin McCorry of Belfast visited the United States in December of 1972 and reported "that 1973 is going to be a difficult year for the friends of the struggle for democracy and justice in Ireland." The *Irish Freedom News*, January 20, 1973, reported "the indifference of American Catholics and especially Irish American Catholics to the oppression of Roman Catholics in Northern Ireland is disappointing but it is not surprising. The news media has so distorted the crisis that most Americans are bewildered into indifference." The NAIF probably has very little political influence among the New York Irish. For example, despite its strong criticism of the Nixon Administration, a strong majority of Irish Catholics in New York voted for Nixon in 1972. (Possibly due to the President's anti-abortion and pro-parochiaid policies.)

Many Catholic diocesan papers have editorially supported the civil rights movement and endorsed nonviolent action on behalf of Ulster Catholics. Rev. Daniel Lyons, editor-at-large of the conservative Catholic weekly *Twin Circle* has been especially prominent in publicizing the Catholic position in the press. In an interview with *Religious News Service* (February 15, 1972) Rev. Lyons stated that "terrorist war must give way to a well-organized propaganda assault." Let the world know of the plight of the Catholics and Ulster will be shamed into submission to many of their demands, he seemed to be implying. In a telling letter to the *National Catholic Reporter* (June 22, 1973) Lyons said: "Catholics in Northern Ireland must rely on the Catholic press in this country to come to their defense. The secular papers seldom mention the *main violence* in that unhappy country, i.e., job discrimination against the 500,000 Catholics (author's emphasis)." It seems incredible to me that Father Lyons, after viewing the bombed-out rubble, the destruction, the maiming and killing of thousands of people,

140

would refer to job discrimination as the main violence. Furthermore, not all 500,000 Catholics are being discriminated against. The majority of Catholics are gainfully employed, though their unemployment rate in some areas is deplorable.

Even liberal Catholics are getting into the act. The National Association of Laity, which has demanded financial disclosures from the hierarchy and opposed efforts to win government support for parochial schools, adopted this resolution at their July 1972 annual convention in Detroit.

DISCRIMINATION IN NORTHERN IRELAND

Resolved that the National Association of Laity publicly protest the abuse of our kinsmen and coreligionists in Ireland, and petition President Nixon to close the American military base in County Derry and recall all American military personnel from Ireland where they are stationed without consent of the Irish people.

Considerations leading to this resolution were the systematic discrimination in housing and employment against the Catholic population in the six northeastern counties of Ireland, and the denial or abridgement of their civil rights for the past fifty years; and the police state situation in Northern Ireland whereby the Catholic population is deprived of all legal protection whenever the Northern Ireland Special Powers Act is invoked.

The leading American public figure to embrace the Irish Catholic cause is Senator Edward M. Kennedy of Massachusetts. Kennedy cabled his support to the Catholics as early as 1969 and intensified his efforts in 1971.

In October of that year the senior Senator from Massachusetts demanded that British troops leave Ulster and that all of Ireland be reunited. This was a bombshell. The British government regarded it as unwarranted interference in the internal affairs of a sovereign state. The British press was universally critical of such an attack on America's oldest and most trusted ally. Most British politicians hesitated to denounce

141

American policy in Vietnam for ten long years when the rest of the world bitterly critical and disillusioned.

The following is reproduced from the *Congressional Record*, October 20, 1971. It contains Senator Kennedy's address and resolution.

Mr. KENNEDY. Mr. President, I am pleased to join with Senator Abraham Ribicoff in introducing a Senate resolution calling for the immediate withdrawal of British troops from Northern Ireland and the establishment of a united Ireland. An identical resolution is being introduced today in the House of Representatives by Congressman Hugh Carey of Brooklyn.

We believe that the resolution states the only realistic means to end the killing in Northern Ireland, and to bring peace to a land that has given so much to America, a land that has done so much to enrich the history of our own Nation, a land that is suffering so deeply today.

The conscience of America cannot keep silent when men and women of Ireland are dying. Britain has lost its way, and the innocent people of Northern Ireland are the ones who now must suffer. The time has come for Americans of every faith and political persuasion to speak out. We owe ourselves and our sacred heritage no less.

Down through the centuries, the people of Ireland have been forced to wage a continuing and arduous struggle for freedom and equality. For generations, division and despair have scarred the countryside. The ancient right of self-determination has been denied. Often alone, often without notice from others throughout the world, brave men and women of Ireland have given their lives for the principles they hold dear. Millions have been driven from their homes, forced to leave the land they love, obliged to seek a new life in nations where the yoke of repression could not reach.

Today, the Irish struggle again. But now, they are not alone. They have the support of free peoples in every corner of the world. Their cause is just, and the reforms they seek are basic to all democracies worthy of the name.

The crisis now, however, is especially serious, because

142

the hate and bitterness are taking a new and far more drastic turn. Ulster teeters on the brink of a civil war that threatens to engulf all of Ireland. The Government of Ulster rules by bayonet and bloodshed. The struggle today in the ghettos of Londonderry for liberty and the right of self-determination, for principles that should be the birthright of all peoples who call-themselves free men.

In recent months, we have witnessed appalling outbreaks of civil strife in Northern Ireland—the worst in the entire half-century since Ireland was partitioned. The soaring toll of death and violence is uncontrolled. Thousands flee their homes in terror. Businesses are bombed, and factories close down. Barbed wire roadblocks imprison every street corner. Young children stand on curbstones and shout shrill insults filled with hate. A child is slain returning from an errand for his parents. A priest is killed as he kneels over a desperately wounded victim. A lorry backfires, and the driver is cut down in a wanton hail of military bullets. And, weekend headlines in the respected London Sunday Times bring reports of the newest horror—eyewitness accounts of torture and brutality in Ulster detention camps.

The cause of the present crisis is not difficult to find. As the newly formed American Committee for Ulster Justice has eloquently declared:

"British armor patrolling the streets of Ulster towns is the end result of prolonged misrule. It is the result of fifty years of outright discrimination in employment, in housing, and in political representation. It is the result of a sectarian and oppressive police force, and of a judicial and prison system aimed at suppressing a minority. It is the result of a one-third minority deprived of the right to live in dignity in their own country."

The explosive situation in Northern Ireland transcends the traditional feelings of those who believe America ought not to intervene in the affairs of another nation. That principle is utterly without application here. There are ties between America and Ireland that simply cannot be ignored.

As President Kennedy liked to say, America is a nation of immigrants. The Irish yield to none in their contributions

143

to the people and culture of America. The waves of Irish immigrants who sought our shores in the 19th century launched a movement that spanned our continent and changed the course of American history. They say today that Irish blood flows in the veins of one out of every seven Americans. There are more Irishmen in America now than in the Ireland they left behind.

The Irish have had a monumental impact on the America we know today. Wherever we look—in business and the labor movement, in literature and music, in science and religion—and above all in public service at every level of government, we find citizens of Irish descent who helped to make our Nation great.

They built our railroads, dug our coal, erected our buildings and our churches. They organized our unions and our businesses. They fought in all our wars. They gave us giants like Eugene O'Neill and Scott Fitzgerald in the world of literature and drama. Louis Sullivan in architecture; George M. Cohan and Victor Herbert in the field of music; actresses like Helen Hayes; athletes like John L. Sullivan, and Gene Tunney; John McGraw and Connie Mack; pillars of the church like Archbishop Ireland, Cardinal Gibbons, Cardinal Spellman, and Cardinal Cushing; labor leaders like George Meany; military heroes from the Revolution to Vietnam; and political leaders at every level—Federal, State, and local—whose dedication helped ensure the growth and stability of our Nation.

But the wearing of the green knows no narrow boundary of religion or nationality. Even without these bonds of blood and history, the deepening tragedy of Ulster today would demand that voices of concerned Americans everywhere be raised against the killing and the violence of Northern Ireland, just as we seek an end to brutality and repression everywhere. But, because the killing and the violence go on in Ireland, the call to action in America is irresistible.

It is our hope, therefore, in introducing this resolution, that every Member of the Senate and House of Representatives will respond to the cry of Ireland in its hour of need, and join us in our call for peace. Together, we can rally the con-

144

science of the world, and thereby bring powerful new pressure for peace.

Alan Paton, the distinguished South African writer, stated the issue eloquently many years ago in terms that draw the contrast sharply between the heritage of freedom we seek to leave our children in America and the heritage of fear that is the plight not only of young black men in South Africa, but of young Catholics in Ulster and oppressed peoples everywhere:

Cry, the beloved country," he said, "for the unborn child that is the inheritor of our fear. Let him not love the earth too deeply. Let him not laugh too gladly when the water runs through his fingers, nor stand too silent when the setting sun makes red the land with fire. Let him not be too moved when the birds of his land are singing, nor give too much of his heart to a mountain or a valley. For fear will rob him of all if he gives too much.

Men have not known that depth of fear in America for more than a hundred years. But they know it today in Northern Ireland, and that is why Americans now must speak.

I have said many times in the past that the basic issue in Northern Ireland is human rights. Until the minority enjoys equal rights with the majority, peace cannot come to Northern Ireland. Equality is the only instrument to erase the hatreds nurtured by years of fear, repression and mistrust. Americans well know that injustice breeds bitterness, and that from this bitterness can come violence at almost any provocation. America has learned that the solution is not repression, the solution is not armed troops, the solution is not barbed wire detention camps. We have found a better way, a way of peace and reconciliation, and we believe that Northern Ireland can reach the same result.

The heart of the solution we offer today is the call for immediate withdrawal of British troops from Ulster and the establishment of a united Ireland. Without a firm commitment to troop withdrawal and unification, there can be no peace in Northern Ireland. The killing will go on, and the intolerable mounting violence will continue.

145

To those who say that the inevitable result of a troop withdrawal will be a blood bath in Northern Ireland, I reply that the blood is upon us now, and the bath is growing more bloody every week. As the resolution states, the only hope for peace is the prompt return of law enforcement to local civilian control in Ulster, in accord with procedures acceptable to all the parties.

Tragically, the Government of Great Britain fails to realize that the presence of British troops in Ulster is compounding the violence instead of contributing to peace. Indeed, the government is moving blindly in the opposite direction. Last week, we learned that another 1,500 British troops are embarking for Northern Ireland. Supposedly, the troops will seal the border to the south, but all they will really seal is yet another step in the escalating violence.

Rarely has there been a clearer example of the well-known truth that those who cannot remember the past are condemned to repeat it. Britain has seen it all before, for the tragedy of Ulster is yet another chapter in the unfolding larger tragedy of the Empire—it is India and Palestine and Cyprus and Africa once again. It is the birth of the Irish Republic in 1920. It is the struggle of men everywhere for the basic rights of freedom and self-determination.

In another sense as well, the tragedy of Ulster is the tragedy of America in Indochina. For Ulster is becoming Britain's Vietnam. Indeed, it is fair to say that Britain stands toward peace in Northern Ireland today where America stood in Southeast Asia in the early nineteen sixties.

The parallel is uncanny. When President Kennedy died, only 120 American soldiers had been killed in action in Vietnam between 1961 and 1963. This week we learned that 128 persons had died in Northern Ireland in the 2 years of bitter violence that have gripped that land since British troops first arrived in 1969.

We know that the years from 1961 to 1963 were only an early chapter in the American horror of Vietnam. We know the tragedy that unfolded there in later years—45,000 Americans have now died in the war; hundreds of thousands of North and South Vietnamese soldiers have been killed;

146

millions of innocent civilians have died, and millions more are homeless refugees in their own country.

Surely, if Britain sees and understands the parallel, we can avoid a repetition of Vietnam in Ulster. The most hopeful sign I see is the growing volume of press reports that the mass of British people themselves see the issue more clearly than their government. A recent poll, taken in September, reveals that fully 59 percent of the British public want to end the killing by bringing British troops home from Ulster now. Simple humanity demands no less. Without that step, no peace is possible, and there can be no settlement of all the other issues.

It is equally clear that the true answer to these other issues is the unification of Ireland, the overall goal we seek in our Senate resolution. America learned a century ago that our Nation, divided against itself, could not stand. The qustion now for Ireland is whether the people there will accept that lesson without enduring a civil war like our own. I believe deeply that they will. In 1918, the people of Ireland voted 81 percent in favor of an independent Republic. If only the cruel and constant irritation of the British military presence is withdrawn, Ireland can be whole again.

Some have urged that the only route for Britain out of Ulster is the solution used by President De Gaulle to end the Algerian war. Just as De Gaulle opened the arms of France to welcome home those Frenchmen who felt they could not live in a free Algeria, so, it is urged, Britain could open its arms to any Protestants in Ulster who feel they could not live in a united Ireland.

But I do not believe that such a solution will be necessary, at least on any wholesale scale for the Protestants who live in Ulster now. It is far more likely that, once the commitment to unification is made, the 500,000 Catholics and 1 million Protestants of Ulster will work together in a new Ireland, to create the sort of political and social arrangements under which both can live and work in peace together, with full and mutual respect for the rights of all. Anyone who doubts that truth need only examine the extraordinary record of equality, tolerance, and religious freedom

147

compiled by the overwhelming 2.7 million Catholic majority in the Republic of Ireland toward the 300,000 Protestant minority there. Any threat the Protestants of Ulster feel is far more a result of guilt over their discrimination against the Catholics of Ulster than a realistic fear of future discrimination against themselves at the hands of the Catholics of a united Ireland.

In addition to the calls for the withdrawal of British troops and the establishment of a united Ireland, there are four other major actions that our Senate resolution proposes:

First, there must be an end to the current internment policy and the simultaneous release of all the prisoners who have been arrested and imprisoned under that brutal and arbitrary policy. For it is a policy that is nothing more nor less than mass arrest and open-ended imprisonment on the basis of mere suspicion, without trial or even the most rudimentary safeguards of fundamental justice and due process of law.

Originally, many of the prisoners were held on HMS *Maidstone,* a prison ship anchored off the Irish coast. Today, more than a hundred prisoners are confined in Crumlin Road in Belfast, and nearly 200 are held at Long Kesh outside the city, a place that many observers say has all the hallmarks of a concentration camp.

These men are political prisoners in the true sense of the word. The internment order was issued on August 9 by Prime Minister Brian Faulkner of Northern Ireland. It was issued under the so-called Special Powers Act, whose blanket language authorized Faulkner to "take all such steps and issue all such orders as may be necessary for preserving the peace and maintaining order."

To the Catholic minority in Ulster, the Special Powers Act is the symbol of their repression. Their deepest fears have been borne out by the internment order issued under it. Indeed, it is fair to say that the act itself probably contains the most sweeping single grant of arbitrary power in any democratic nation in the Western World.

The act itself has become a model for repressive regimes throughout the world. It was cited with approval as recently as 1963 by Prime Minister Vorster in South Africa. In the course of proposing a series of restrictive measures for South

148

Africa, including the infamous 90-day detention law. Vorster argued that he would be willing to exchange all the authority he sought for one clause of Northern Ireland's Special Powers Act.

There can be no justification for the application of the act in Northern Ireland. Internment is a cruel and abhorrent policy. The random midnight roundup of suspects on the night of August 9 this year—the knock on the door, the violent entry, the arrest in the dark of night—rank as yet another flagrant example of the repression of the Ulster minority.

The government said the detention order was aimed at both Protestant and Catholic extremists, but 300 Catholics have been arrested, and not a single Protestant. The only real result of the internment policy has been to inflame the population more deeply, and to trigger a new and far more terrifying escalation of the violence—in the first 7 weeks that followed the issuance of the internment order, 17 British soldiers, 35 civilians, and one policeman were killed, and the end is not in sight. Surely, the first step on the route back to sanity in Ulster must be the revocation of the order and the release of the prisoners.

Second, the resolution calls for full respect for the civil rights of all the people of Northern Ireland, and the end of all political, social, economic, and religious discrimination that now exists in Ulster. The crisis in Northern Ireland is a lesson to the world that religious intolerance can run just as deep and be just as cruel and violent as racial discrimination. I fully support the struggle for equal rights by the oppressed Catholic minority in Ulster, just as I support the rights of black Americans and other minorities wherever they are oppressed in the United States, whether in Jackson, Miss., or in Roxbury, Mass. For too long, Great Britain, one of the noblest bastions of freedom and equality in the history of the world, has allowed some of the most blatant and individious imaginable discriminations to flourish on its Ulster doorstep. The time has come to end them.

Third, the resolution calls for implementation of the many basic reforms promised by the Governments of Great Britain and Northern Ireland since 1968, including the re-

149

forms specifically promised in the area of law enforcement, housing, employment, and voting rights. Time and again, in recent years, the people of Ulster have heard the promise of reform, but they have never had performance. Landmarks like the O'Neil reforms of 1968 and the Downing Street Declaration of 1969, lie forgotten on the drawing boards. The time has come for movement on all of these promised actions.

Fourth, and finally, the resolution calls for the dissolution of the Parliament of Northern Ireland. Today, the Parliament of Northern Ireland has become one of the overriding symbols of oppression of the Ulster minority. For generations, the Parliament at Stormont has been the tool of Protestant domination in Ulster, and I can find no justification for its continuance. Instead, pending the overall settlement of the Ulster issue, the people of Northern Ireland should be governed directly from Westminster—the British Parliament in London—just like every other British subject. There has never been a valid rationale for the interposition of the Stormont Parliament between the Ulster people and Westminster. It is an artificial barrier between the people and their government, and the sooner this parliamentary thorn is removed, the better.

We believe that the sum of these proposals offers the only real hope for the freedom of the people of Northern Ireland and an end to the reign of violence and terror that threatens to consume that land. No one doubts that Ireland stands today on the brink of a massive civil war. The spectre we face is nothing less then the senseless destruction of Ireland herself. No American who loves Ireland or who remembers her proud and noble history can stand silent in the face of the tragedy and horror now unfolding in Ulster.

Ireland has given much to America, and we owe her much in return. Perhaps, if America can see the issue clearly, Britain will understand.

The immortal words of the Irish martyr, Robert Emmet, are as current today as when he spoke then from the dock in 1803. Condemned to death for his role in a Dublin uprising that year, he addressed the court in words as familiar to every schoolchild of Ireland as Lincoln's Address at Gettysburg is to the children of America:

"Let no man write my epitaph; for as no man who know my motives dares now vindicate them, let not prejudice or ignorance asperse them. Let them and me rest in obscurity and peace: and my tomb remain uninscribed, and my memory in oblivion, until other times and other men can do justice to my character. When my country takes her place among the nations of the earth, then and not till then, let my epitaph be written."

SENATE RESOLUTION 180—SUBMISSION OF A RESOLUTION RELATING TO THE VIOLENCE IN NORTHERN IRELAND

(Referred to the Committee on Foreign Relations.)

S.RES. 180

Whereas, the continuing violence and bloodshed in Northern Ireland is a cause of the deepest concern to Americans of all faiths and political persuasions;

Whereas, the cause of the present conflict may be traced to the systematic and deliberate discrimination in housing, employment, political representation and educational opportunities practiced by the governmental authorities of Northern Ireland against the minority there;

Whereas, the governments of the United Kingdom and of Northern Ireland have failed to end the bloodshed and have failed to establish measures to meet the legitimate grievances of this minority;

Whereas, continued repression and lack of fundamental reforms in Northern Ireland threaten to prolong and escalate the conflict and the denial of civil liberties: Now, therefore be it.

Resolved, That the Senate of the United States expresses its deepest concern over the present situation in Northern Ireland, and in accord with fundamental concepts of nondiscrimination, fairness, democracy, self-determination and justice, requests the Government of the United States at the highest level to urge the immediate implementation of the following actions:

1. Termination of the current internment policy and

151

the simultaneous release of all persons detained thereunder.

2. Full respect for the civil rights of all the people of Northern Ireland, and the termination of all political, social, economic and religious discrimination.

3. Implementation of the reforms promised by the Government of the United Kingdom since 1968, including reforms in the fields of law enforcement, housing, employment, and voting rights.

4. Dissolution of the Parliament of Northern Ireland.

5. Withdrawal of all British forces from Northern Ireland and the institution of law enforcement and criminal justice under local control acceptable to all parties.

6. Convening of all interested parties for the purposes of accomplishing the unification of Ireland.

The *London Times* was acidly critical. It published this editorial.

Sen. Edward Kennedy expresses surprise that there should have been so strong a reaction over here to his observations about the Irish question. He should try to understand that what he professes to see, from the other side of the Atlantic, as a struggle for liberation from colonial oppression looks, from the closer range of the United Kingdom, like an armed conspiracy against the state: an indiscriminately violent attempt to annex territory and transfer its sovereignty against the strong and stable wishes of two-thirds of the people living in that territory.

When someone who is understood to be in the field for presidential office in the United States elects to describe the aggressors in that conflict as being engaged "in the struggle of men everywhere for the basic rights of freedom and self-determination," he must not expect to be heard in polite silence by those who, defending the integrity of the state at some cost of lives and resources, believe themselves to be defending the freedom and right of self-determination of the people of Northern Ireland.

For our part we do not dispute Sen. Kennedy's entitlement to express what view of the conflict in Northern Ireland he pleases, or to add it to the list of oppressions the world over concerning which he appoints himself the conscience of free men. He has as much right as anyone else called Kennedy to demand the unification of Ireland and to propose simple ways of bringing it about. The good sense or lack of it which he displays in that regard is primarily a matter between him and the electors of the United States.

Exception must be taken however to Sen. Kennedy's suggestion that the principle of non-intervention of one nation in the internal affairs of another is "utterly without application here" because of the migratory ties between the United States and Ireland. That doctrine, giving the United States rights of intervention in the affairs of a dozen states or more and vice versa, would change very much for the worse the conduct of relations between states in the western world.

Another point which needs to be made is this. Sen. Kennedy is distressed by the shedding of blood in Ulster. Believing that the bloodshed is attributable to the presence of troops in that part of the United Kingdom, he has called for their immediate withdrawal. The evidence of history and contemporary observation of the province make it highly probable that the immediate withdrawal of troops would precipitate civil war between the communities in Ulster. From the ashes of that conflict a united Irish republic might or might not arise. But let neither Sen. Kennedy nor anyone else, in proposing a military withdrawal, pretend that it would do other than bring more death and destruction to the province.

Senator Kennedy retorted on October 22:

Sir, I am surprised and somewhat puzzled by the intensity of the reaction in Great Britain against my Senate resolution calling for the immediate withdrawal of British troops from Ulster and the unification of Ireland.

As my remarks on the Senate floor make clear, I do not believe the Ulster issue can fairly be called the "internal affair" of Britain alone. I do believe that the continuing presence of British troops in Ulster is compounding the violence

153

instead of contributing to peace, and I also believe that the turmoil will not end until law enforcement is again returned to local control.

Even were I neither Irish nor Catholic, I would feel compelled to speak out against the violence and brutality in Northern Ireland, just as I have spoken out again and again in recent years on the violence and brutality in areas like Vietnam, Biafra, the Middle East and East Bengal. I shall continue to speak out on the Ulster question until the killing and oppression end, and I shall urge others in every nation to do the same, so that together we can rally the conscience of the world.

But the passionate response directed against my remarks has, I think, at least in part, a basis of another sort. It is difficult to believe that my proposal would have generated such fervor if Britain, one of the great symbols of freedom and democracy to us Americans, did not have a guilty conscience over Ulster.

Sincerely,
Edward M. Kennedy
United States Senate
Washington, DC
October 22, 1971

This tempest eventually died down and the Kennedy resolution did not pass the Senate. Many thoughtful observers regarded this incident as a tragic blunder on Kennedy's part. Others judged it a cynical attempt to solidify a religio-ethnic bloc for future political use. I regard it as a lack of prudence and judgment and a misguided exercise in adventurism. The last thing Americans want today is to get involved in another overseas conflict, whether in the Middle East, Southeast Asia, or Northern Ireland. We don't want another Vietnam on the Irish Sea. Neither do we want an increase in religious or ethnic strife here at home.

While this resolution failed, other Irish-American organizations continued to agitate for the Catholic cause. The American Committee for Ulster Justice issued this statement on "The U.S. Role in the Irish Question."

Newsletter of the American Committee for Ulster Justice, June 1, 1972.

The United States Role in the Irish Question

Channel 13's public forum T.V. program "The Advocates" recently debated the motion 'that the United States should support the unification of Ireland.' The format was such that counsel for and against the proposition questioned outstanding spokesmen of the major parties to the conflict in Northern Ireland. The television audience was invited to vote for or against the motion by mailing their ballots to the T.V. station. The result of the ballot showed the American public overwhelmingly in favor of support for the unification of Ireland as 77% of the more than 15,000 votes cast were affirmative.

There are many reasons why the people of the United States and the government should be interested in helping to find a solution to the present conflict in Northern Ireland. The following presents some of the reasons, but fundamentally the U.S. must interest itself on the grounds of kinship, our own colonial past and the fact that the presence of violence anywhere is a festering sore that has a habit in these days of instant communication of spreading.

On the grounds of kinship, there are as many as 40,000,000 Americans whose ancestors (one or more of them) came from Ireland. Some twelve of the United States Presidents have had Irish ancestors including Presidents Kennedy and Nixon. The contribution of the Irish and their descendants to the building of this great nation is a story fully documented and well known to the American people. In the case of the affinity of the U.S. with the State of Israel many specific economic, military and diplomatic steps have been taken to aid and support her in times of danger. The plight of the Jewish community in the Soviet Union, surely by other yardsticks of measurement an internal matter for the Moscow authorities to resolve, is a topic of discussion in President Nixon's trip to the Kremlin. The State Department has apparently overlooked the argument in this case that the matter of the Jewish community is a domestic affair of the Soviet Union. Are not the grounds of kinship as strong in the case of Ireland as in the case of Israel?

155

The violence in N.I. is the final chapter in Ireland's seemingly eternal struggle against British colonialism. The United States, which itself was the first colony of Britain to successfully initiate its independence, must look with sympathy on the fight of the people who of all the nations on earth are most identified with the historical movement of national liberation and political independence. Benjamin Franklin understood the position of the Irish people and when he addressed the Irish Parliament soliciting their aid he received their wholehearted support for the enterprise then astir in England's North American colonies. Five thousand of General Washington's troops were Irish, including three of his Generals. Ireland inspired the downfall of the greatest colonial empire ever created. Does she not have the right to the sympathy and concern of those she helped liberate from the same cruel yoke?

The United States has interceded in one way or another, without the involvement of troops in many disputes between states in recent years. President Nixon has sent Secretary of State Rogers to find some basis for agreement and the lessening of tensions in the Middle East. President Johnson sent Cyrus Vance to mediate in the Cyprus crisis and his Assistant Secretary of State for Latin America mediated between Great Britain and Honduras in 1964 after both nations broke off diplomatic relations over the question of British Honduras.

While the United States is maintaining at great cost a large standing army in Europe under our committment to NATO, the British Army has more than 15,500 of its Army personnel, not to mention all of its intelligence and other services, concentrated in the colonial war in Northern Ireland. A recent edition of the *London Economist* recognized that such a development has seriously undermined Great Britain's commitment to its NATO allies.

The United States need not involve itself in any military solution in Northern Ireland, but rather the influence of friendly persuasion should be used to convince the United Kingdom that the only permanent solution lies in a Free, United and Independent Ireland.

156

Some members of Congress continue to attempt to use the Ulster tragedy for obvious political gain. Rep. Mario Biaggi, a Democrat from New York City and the Conservative Party candidate for Mayor of New York in 1973, encouraged his colleagues to keep the Northern Ireland issue before the American public. He placed the following remarks in the *Congressional Record:*

ATROCITIES IN NORTHERN IRELAND
HON. MARIO BIAGGI
OF NEW YORK
IN THE HOUSE OF REPRESENTATIVES
Thursday, March 1, 1973

Mr. BIAGGI. Mr. Speaker, stories of atrocities occurring daily in Northern Ireland are beginning to fall upon deaf ears. Too many individuals the world over are now turning their eyes from the conflict raging constantly in Belfast.

Unless the day-to-day horror of their situation can be dramatized on a regular basis, we run the risk of allowing the bloodshed to continue while peaceful nations stand by in apathy. It is the responsibility of the Members of this House to see to it that the true story of what is happening in Northern Ireland is kept before the eyes of all Americans.

It is for this reason, Mr. Speaker, that I would like to read into the *Record* the heart-rending letter which Paul Nathanson, an English citizen whose family was directly affected by the ongoing Belfast tragedy submitted to the editor of the London Evening News. He speaks of 12-year-old Philip Rafferty—a cousin of the Nathanson family—who was recently abducted, hooded, and shot through the head. This frail, asthmatic child was just one of the hundreds and hundreds of innocent victims who have been chosen by heartless murderers for senseless execution.

Mr. Speaker, if the people of the United States and their elected representatives succumb to indifference in the face of such an outrage, then we must share responsibioity for the brutal death of Philip Rafferty. I would encourage my col-

157

leagues to join in the effort aimed at keeping the Northern Ireland issue before the American public. If the pressure of international opinions can contribute to bringing about peace in Belfast, then we must register our sense of outrage at the slaughter of such defenseless victims as Philip Rafferty.

Mr. Nathanson's letter to the editor follows:

LONDON, ENGLAND

SIR: I am a Jew. I came from Austria to England as a little boy over 30 years ago when six million of my people were put to death.

I recall among my murdered family a cousin, with whom I shared my early childhood, who was made to give up his life for being a Jew in Hitler's gas chambers at the age of 12.

My wife was born in England. Her father was Irish, Her mother is of the same background as me—we shared the same six million dead.

My wife and I have two little girls. Now, nearly 30 years after the Second World War, the journey to the moon and other various wars, my little girls have just lost their own little cousin.

He was a small, frail boy who suffered from asthma and who had a Mum and Dad, Brother, sister, uncle and aunts.

One day while the kids played, he was abducted, hooded, shot through the head and his body dumped.

Why did he die? What had he done? For what cause did he die? Why? Why?

Were the Jews murdered throughout the ages for the religion they were born into? Was Philip murdered because he was a Catholic? Did he die for Ireland? For Glory? For God? O no!

No, never!

I am a Jew. I am alive! To You who murdered my people, to You who kill in other corners of the world, to You who murdered a terrified innocent child because of his Christian label, I say:

"Philip Rafferty, and all other 'Philips' whatever their creed, do not die as heroes or martyrs, nor do they die for a cause—they die in vain—for nothing!

158

"You murdered a child for no reason!

"One day, when you will have to justify your deeds, there will be no defence—for any of us. And only then, when this is realized, will Philip Rafferty have died for a cause."

I am dear Sir,

PAUL NATHANSON.

The Protestants also have their supporters in the U.S., but on a much more modest scale. Rev. Carl McIntire's Twentieth Century Reformation Movement in Collingwood, New Jersey, is the main source of support for Ian Paisley's movement in Ulster. Paisley has made several speaking tours of the U.S., under McIntyre's sponsorship, and has spoken at the annual summer conferences at the Christian Admiral Hotel in Cape May, New Jersey.

International Christian Relief, an arm of McIntire's International Council of Christian Churches (an extreme right-wing counterpart of the World Council of Churches) launched a campaign in September 1969 to aid the Protestant Cause in Ulster. ICR opened an office in Belfast to disburse the funds to "suffering Protestants." When the campaign was announced in the *Christian Beacon* (September 4, 1969) this strange comment was made: "These funds will also be used to help the Protestants in the South of Ireland, who can no longer bear the persecutions and privations which are theirs and desire to move to the North. They will also help the Roman Catholics in the North who desire to go to the Irish Republic." No estimates of the amount raised have been issued.

The Orange Order has about 2,000 members in the U.S. Its Grand Master is Mr. William Best, an Ulster native and proprietor of Bestway Travel Agency in New York City. I have met Mr. Best and he is a very personable, articulate and tolerant man who feels Ulster has been misrepresented. Mr. Best has formed the Ulster-Irish Society to present the Protestant side of the debate. It brings influential Ulstermen to America.

The Northern Ireland Service Council is another group of Americans with close ties to Ulster. Its Rochester, New York,

159

chairman Mr. John Garland seeks to improve Ulster's image in the U.S. press. His home was attacked and damaged in early 1973 because of his pro-Ulster activities.

Two Americans are engaged in an unusual aspect of the Ulster conflict. Hurst Hannum, a 27-year-old Pennsylvanian with a Berkeley law degree and James C. Heaney, a Buffalo lawyer, represent Catholic clients before the European Commission on Human Rights in Strasbourg, France. Hannum, who lives and works in Belfast, won a major victory in May, 1973, when the Commission announced that it "has admitted for further investigation" complaints brought by seven Catholic men against British security forces for alleged ill-treatment.

Mr. Hannum and a Belfast colleague Kevin Boyle charged that the British brutally beat and tortured the seven men, five of whom are still held in prison or detention centers. These charges are extremely serious and well documented. In October 1972 the Commission agreed to investigate similar charges brought by the Irish government in Dublin. British government authorities are so concerned that they are sending a team of top lawyers to argue the case in Strasbourg.

Mr. Hannum is also preparing a brief for the United Nations Human Rights Commission, which alleges widespread torture and anti-Catholic discrimination. Hannum has no Irish ancestry and regards himself as essentially neutral vis-a-vis Ulster. But he sincerely believes that British security forces have violated international standards of prisoner treatment. If his charges stick, it will severely damage the credibility of the British presence in Ulster.

Are America's churches doing anything constructive for Ulster's moderate, peaceful majority? Is any help going to the victims of violence? There is some burgeoning assistance. A group of 40 young Catholic and Protestant volunteers worked in Ulster during the summer of 1973 in a program designed to encourage interdenominational cooperation. The group is called Colleagues from American Churches, which may be incorporated as a nonprofit organization. Most of the volunteers

160

are college and seminary students. The informal leader of the group is Father David Bowman, who serves as Catholic representative to the National Council of Churches.

In November 1972, Bishop John J. Dougherty, chairman of the U.S. Catholic Bishops Committee for Social Development and Peace, called upon all American Catholic Bishops to give their personal assistance for the rebuilding of homes destroyed in Belfast's civil strife.

Religious News Service (Nov. 14, 1972) reported that assistance for Northern Ireland carried a "top priority" at the Vatican. Father David Bowman learned from Monsignor Joseph Gremillion, American-born secretary to the Vatican Justice and Peace Commission, that the Vatican was "embarrassed" by Ulster Catholics who resorted to terrorism. Bowman referred to Ulster as "the deepest wound in the body of Christ."

Pentecost Sunday, June 10, 1973, was declared a day of prayer for peace in Ulster by the World Council of Churches and the Vatican. This "Ecumenical Initiative" was strongly supported throughout the U.S.

On March 16, 1973, the executive heads of the National Council of Churches, the National Conference of Catholic Bishops and the Synagogue Council of America urged that Americans cut off all contributions to groups that support violence in Ulster. They declared: "We recommend that financial support be limited to denominational, ecumenical and interreligious collections which are transmitted to counterpart agencies in Ireland so that American funds will be used not for purposes of destruction but for the building of a just and compassionate society in Northern Ireland. We believe it is a very special scandal when people fight and kill one another in the name of religion." Well said.

ULSTER

The dark eleventh hour
Draws on and sees us sold
To every evil power
We fought against of old,
Rebellion, rapine, hate,
Oppression, wrong, and greed
Are loosed to rule our fate,
By England's act and deed.

The faith in which we stand,
The laws we made and guard,
Our honour, lives and land,
Are given for reward
To Murder done by night,
To Treason taught by day,
To folly, sloth, and spite,
And we are thrust away.

The blood our fathers spilt,
Our love, our toils, our pains.
Are counted as for guilt,
And only bind our chains,
Before an Empire's eyes
The traitor claims his price.
What need of further lies?
We are the sacrifice.

We asked no more than leave
To reap where we had sown,
Through good and ill to cleave
To our own flag and throne.
Now England's shot and steel
Beneath that flag must show
How loyal hearts should kneel
To England's oldest foe.

We know the war prepared
On every peaceful home,
We know the hells declared
For such as serve not Rome—
The terror, threats, and dread
In market, hearth, and field—
We know, when all is said,
We perish if we yield.

Believe, we dare not boast,
Believe, we do not fear—
We stand to pay the cost
In all that men hold dear.
What answer from the North?
One law, one land, one throne.
If England drive us forth
We shall not fall alone.

Rudyard Kipling.

Perhaps the most famous poem ever written about Ulster was Rudyard Kipling's "Ulster", which was written in 1912 as a paean to Ulster's Loyalists.

9.   Summing Up

To summarize what I believe to be true about Northern Ireland:

1. The Scarman, Hunt, and Cameron Commission reports to the British government show that Roman Catholics have suffered some discrimination in housing, employment, and local government franchise. On the other hand, Roman Catholics received a majority of public housing allocations since 1945 and there has been some discrimination against Protestants in some small, largely Catholic border towns. Because of the historic employment "pinch" in Ulster, jobs were at a premium and it seemed natural for each side to discriminate in favor of its own people. The Catholic unemployment rate is much higher than the Protestant, reaching an estimated 47 percent in the Ballymurphy area of Belfast today. The Stormont government, under prodding from London, sought to rectify these conditions by establishing a system of need for housing allocations and by enforcing nondiscrimination in the public employment sector. This discrimination, however, did not justify the use of violence to bring about change. The Civil Rights Movement, of course, played a part in awakening people to the discrimination problem.

2. The dual system of education has reinforced and perpetuated existing divisions in society. My most depressing experience was watching British soldiers patroling a mixed

neighborhood when the two school systems closed for the day. Protestant and Catholic school children walked on separate sides of the street surrounded by soldiers whose presence was absolutely essential to prevent the eruption of violence.

3. The role of the churches has not been very constructive. They have all too often emphasized insular, narrow interests rather than the common good. The nation is reaping a bitter harvest because of the negative, hostile manner in which the churches view each other. The churches have, in fact, deeply embarrassed Christianity throughout the world by their involvement in the Northern Ireland tragedy.

4. A plethora of laws, ameliorative, punitive, and preventive, have not been able to reconcile deeply divided communities. The problem of religious segregation is so deep-seated that laws as such have only a limited influence.

5. Northern Ireland is still on the brink of chaos, though the threat of civil war has probably been reduced. The Assembly elections, though disappointly sectarian, at least returned a solid majority who are publicly committed to power sharing between Protestants and Catholics and who are willing to give the new system of government a try.

6. Northern Ireland, because a majority of people wish it so, will remain a part of the United Kingdom. British security forces will remain for the forseeable future.

7. The Protestant community is justified in wanting to maintain the constitutional link with Britain, which guarantees individual liberties to a greater extent than the Republic of Ireland.

8. If the concept of a united Ireland is ever to have any validity or reality, the government of the Irish Republic must extricate itself from the excessive influence of the Catholic hierarchy. This will necessitate far-reaching changes and should include a nonsectarian school system, provisions for civil divorce and family planning, abolition of the infamous censorship laws, and allowance for interfaith adoptions. The Roman Catholic Church should also abolish its restrictive intermar-

riage requirements as a major step toward easing intercreedal tensions. Similarly, the Protestant clergy in the North should be willing to see the Sunday "blue laws" abolished. In some parts of Ulster even children's playgrounds are locked on Sunday. The development of a truly pluralistic society in both the North and South is a prerequisite to any eventual unity.

9. It is impossible to blame one side more than the other. A majority of the dead and displaced have been Roman Catholics in a two-thirds Protestant land. The bitterness engendered in the last four years is incalculable and it is frightening to contemplate what the next generation will do.

10. The vast majority of Ulster people are decent, law-abiding and moderate, but their voices are drowned out by the sound and fury of the extremists. The "silent" majority are at a disadvantage because they do not employ the methods of the extremists. There should be some legal way of "quarantining" those who have a vested interest in violence. Terrorism must cease. When society is faced by anarchy, repression inevitably occurs. Both the Scylla of anarchy and Charybidis of repression are horrible alternatives but one leads to the other, as the day follows the night. If the terrorists don't cease their activities, the ultimate result will be far worse for all sides than even the present.

11. The media have sensationalized and presented an essentially negative view of Ulster. They have failed to point out that Ulster's gross national product is steadily rising, industrial production is up 11 percent, and unemployment is down from 8.2. percent to 6.7 percent. When positive, hopeful events occur, the media should publicize them too.

12. Ultimate solution of the Ulster situation is still hampered by the fact that one-third of the population rejects the legitimacy, the very existence of the State in which they live. This makes the whole situation almost insoluble. Therefore, amelioration must occur in stages as specific problems are tackled individually.

13. As far as bigotry is concerned, the Protestant variety is

more virulent and sustained. It is directed at Catholicism as a religion and Catholics as a religious community. Catholic bigotry is more nationalistic in nature and is directed against alleged British colonialism. Protestants and Protestantism are generally ignored in Catholic literature, which is a subtle form of bigotry.

14. The IRA (both the Provos and Officials) still commands considerable support in the Belfast and Londonderry Catholic ghettoes. No guerrilla force can exist for long in an area without indigenous support. Much of the original support has been alienated by the violence and the number of innocent people who have suffered as a result of it.

The IRA has some support among the Catholic clergy but it has declined considerably, as recent condemnations by parish priests and the Cardinal attests. When the Vatican endorsed the White Paper and explicitly condemned terrorism in the spring of 1973, the IRA criticized the Pope as "misinformed." All of this probably seems confusing to observers and the confusion is compounded when IRA thugs are given well-publicized Catholic funerals. It is probably true to say that there is little religious influence of any brand in the IRA today.

15. Ulster was not the repressive state it has been depicted. It had many inequities (which country doesn't?) but civil and religious liberties were maintained to a higher degree than most other nations in the world. There were problems of fair law enforcement, but the fact that the Civil Rights Movement could demonstrate forcefully indicated that the system was resilient and subject to change. Many policies of the Unionist government were short-sighted and timid, however.

16. The new Irish government of Prime Minister Liam Cosgrave appears to be acting very responsibly and may help to achieve peace in Ulster through farsighted conciliatory policies. This may be one of the most hopeful signs.

What can be done to end the tragic strife in Northern Ireland? Here are some suggestions:

166

1. The schools could become reconciling institutions. If both sides could take the courageous first step and agree to primary-school integration, the effect could be positive. Certain problems would have to be worked out. Catholic and Protestant teachers are trained in separate colleges and are divided by their respective professional associations. Problems in textbooks, interpretations of history, and the place of the Irish language in the curriculum would have to be resolved. Because of the prominence of religion in the present curricula, a "released time" program might be a useful temporary expedient, with clergy from both sides teaching religion classes at a specific time. These changes would reduce the cost of duplicate separate school systems and contribute to interconfessional peace.

2. Northern Ireland must work out her destiny in the present political framework. The British White Paper seems to be a reasonable compromise which will insure both Protestant majority rule and greater Roman Catholic participation in government. Justice must be granted to the minority in any truly democratic state. Those who advocate a united Ireland by force, or an independent Ulster state a la Rhodesia are misguided and malevolent.

3. A nonsectarian, inclusive political party system should replace the present narrowly based parties. The Unionist Party, for example, should have welcomed Catholic support in the late 1950's. When it refused, the political situation polarized further. The parties now existing are so tarnished by the past that a new alliance based on common objectives is needed.

4. Church leaders should meet regularly to discuss interfaith problems and tensions before they explode into violence. Both sides should attempt to revise their catechetical and apologetical literature to reflect a deeper appreciation and understanding of the other faith. There is more to unite Christians than to divide them.

5. The Special Powers Act, which gives the government authority to arrest and intern people suspected of criminal of-

fenses and then to hold them without trial or formal charges for an indefinite period of time, should be abolished. This is an affront to civil liberties and has been applied almost exclusively against the Catholic community.

6. Americans should cease sending financial aid to extremists on either side in Northern Ireland. Money collected in the United States is often used for the purchase of weapons, rather than for food or clothing. This misguided romanticism is disruptive to the law-abiding peaceful majority in Ulster.

7. Since economic maldistribution is one of Ulster's plights and unemployment is so widespread in certain Catholic areas, the British government should embark on a massive aid program to reduce substantially the above problems. The development of more industry west of the Bann River and in the depressed areas of Belfast is essential. Of course, the level of violence must be reduced or halted altogether so that industrialists will feel secure about relocating to Ulster. Ulster terrosim has already cost the British Government $275 million, including $115 million in property and personal injury compensation.

8. The Catholic Church should cease giving the impression of being a state within a state. Catholic schools should at least give elemental acts of loyalty to the government which provides 95 percent of its budget. Flying the flag, singing the national anthem and inculcating principles of civil respect are essential. The Church should also send a chaplain to the new Assembly, which it failed to do for Stormont for almost 50 years. The above are to some extent predicated on absolutely fair treatment accorded Catholics by the Protestant majority and the government. When people are treated justly, I believe they will respond.

9. Absolute nondiscrimination in all employment and housing should be guaranteed by law and enforced. A separate body of government could deal with problems as they arise. Perhaps the Community Relations Commission could be expanded and strengthened. I do not favor a quota system,

which is unworkable and may lead to reverse discrimination, but I feel that patterns of discrimination can be identified and rectified.

10. Because of the danger of escalating religious strife to England and Scotland, British security forces should gradually withdraw as soon as the dangers of civil war, sectarian massacres, or terrorism have been sustantially reduced. Unfortunately, this may be a long time. The British public are growing restive and disillusioned by the prolonged agony and the savage deaths of 200 British soldiers. We Americans know what a festering sore the Vietnam War became as it was prolonged and prolonged far beyond what the majority of Americans probably wanted.

11. Even after eventual troop withdrawals, Britain (i.e. the Westminster government) should maintain effective control over police and security until a greater degree of mutual trust between the communities is developed.

12. The Irish Republic's government should clamp down and crush IRA terrorists once and for all. It would also be helpful if the Republic's Constitution could be amended to delete the passage which claims control over the six counties of Ulster. This would reduce tensions and fears in the North. A new extradition treaty should be signed between the Republic and Ulster.

13. Close cooperation in tourism and trade should be developed between the Republic and Ulster.

There's a line from the beautiful Bob Dylan song "Blowin' in the Wind" that can be applied to the tragic events in Ulster, "How many deaths will it take until he knows that too many people have died?" What is desperately needed among both Protestants and Catholics is the realization of common humanity shared by both sides. There can be no Protestant victory or Catholic victory, but only a victory for human understanding and justice.

Many say that the Irish, like the Spanish, have a penchant for extremism, an inability to compromise. I doubt whether this is an intrinsic Irish national characteristic but I do believe that the development of a tolerant spirit is an essential prerequisite for peace. I believe Christians have a special obligation to work for peace and reconciliation within society.

Furthermore, openness to change is another requirement for mature adaptation to our often overwhelming time in history. Change is not pleasant; it is often painful, but one thing is certain: it is inevitable. Public opinion analyst Louis Harris recently wrote of the "anguish" of change in our own United States during the last decade. Change is a necessary and liberating experience. It cannot be prevented. Though the rapidity of social change often seems bewildering, it is a challenge which can produce national greatness and growth. The alternative is stagnation and decline.

The development of a spirit of brotherhood is Ulster's great challenge for the remainder of this century. As Protestants and Catholics come to know and understand each other as fellow human beings, perhaps they can come to realize the significance of Shakespeare's closing lines in *The Comedy of Errors:*

"We came into the world like brother and brother
And now let's go hand in hand, not one before another."

Bibliography

I   *British Government Documents* (Belfast, Her Majesty's Stationery Office)

The Future of Northern Ireland — 1972

Report of the Advisory Committee on Police in Northern Ireland (Cmd. 535) — 1969

Disturbances in Northern Ireland — 1969 (Cmd. 532)

Northern Ireland Constitutional Proposals (The White Paper) — 1973

Official Publications of the Northern Ireland Information Office, Belfast

Ulster Yearbook — 1972, 1973

Violence and Civil Disturbances in Northern Ireland in 1969 (2 vols.) — 1969 (Cmd. 566)

II   *Books and Pamphlets*

Barritt, David P. and Charles F. Carter, *The Northern Ireland Problem,* Oxford University Press, New York, 1972.

Blanshard, Paul, *The Irish and Catholic Power,* Beacon Press, Boston, 1953.

Boulton, David, *The UVF 1966-73: An Anatomy of Loyalist Rebellion,* Gill & MacMillan, Dublin, 1973.

Boyd, Andrew, *Brian Faulkner and the Crisis of Ulster Unionism,* Anvil Books, Tralee, Ireland, 1972.

171

Boyd, Andrew, *Holy War in Belfast,* Anvil Books, Tralee, Ireland, 1969.

Committee on the Religious Instruction Programme for Secondary Intermediate Schools, *Notes on a Syllabus of Religious Education for Secondary School,* Northern Ireland.

Connery, Donald S., *The Irish,* Simon & Schuster, New York, 1968.

Corkey, The Very Rev. William, *Episode in the History of Protestant Ulster,* Belfast, 1959.

de Paor, Liam, *Divided Ulster,* Penguin, Hammondsworth, England, 1972.

Devlin, Bernadette, *The Price of My Soul,* Alfred Knopf, Inc., New York, 1969.

Dewar, Rev. Dr. M.W. et al, *Orangeism,* Grand Orange Lodge of Ireland, Belfast, 1967.

Dewar, Rev. Dr. M.W., *Why Orangeism?*, Grand Orange Lodge of Ireland, 1959.

Dill, Rev. Edward Marcus, *The Mystery Solved, Or Ireland's Miseries,* Edinburgh, 1852.

Fennell, Desmond, *The Changing Face of Catholic Ireland,* Corpus, Washington, 1968.

Fitzgerald, Garret, *Towards A New Ireland,* Charles Knight & Co., London, 1972.

Fraser, Morris, *Children In Conflict,* Secker & Warburg, London, 1973.

Gallagher, Eric. *A Better Way for Irish Protestants and Roman Catholics* — Belfast, 1973

Gardner, Louis, *Resurgence of The Majority,* Vanguard, Belfast, 1971

Government of Northern Ireland, Ministry of Education, *Public Education, Northern Ireland,* Her Majesty's Stationery Office, Belfast, 1970.

Government of Northern Ireland, Ministry of Education, *General Certificate of Education, Rules and Programme,* Her Majesty's Stationery Office, Belfast, 1973.

172

Gillies, Donald, *In Place of Truth*, Unionist Publicity Dept., Belfast, 1972.

Gray, Tony, *The Orange Order*, The Bodley Head, London, 1972.

Gray, Tony, *Psalms and Slaughter—A Study in Bigotry*, Heinemann, London, 1972.

Griffin, William D. (ed.), *The Irish in America*, Oceana, Dobbs Ferry, New York, 1973.

Harris, Rosemary, *Prejudice and Tolerance in Ulster*, Manchester University Press, Manchester, England, 1972.

Hastings, Max, *Barricades in Belfast: The Fight for Civil Rights in Northern Ireland*, Taplinger, New York, 1970.

Herron, S.S., *The Great Conspiracy to Destroy Ulster*, Distributed by Evangelical Protestant Society, Belfast, 1972.

Jackson, Harold, *The Two Irelands*, Minority Rights Groups, London, 1971.

Lucey, Charles, *Ireland and the Irish*, Doubleday, New York, 1970.

Lee, Gordon and Robert Taylor, *Ulster*, The Economist, London, July 1971.

Limpkin, Clive, *The Battle of Bogside*, Penguin, Baltimore, 1973.

London Sunday Times Insight Team, *Northern Ireland: A Report on the Conflict*, Random House, New York, 1972.

McCarthy, Michael, *Priests and People in Ireland*, Hodges, Figgis & Co., Dublin, 1902.

McCarthy, Michael, *Rome in Ireland*, London, 1904.

McGuire, Maria, *To Take Arms: A Year in the Provisional IRA*, MacMillan, London, 1973.

Magee, Jack, *The Teaching of Irish History in Irish Schools*, NICRC, Belfast 1971.

Manhattan, Avro, *Religious Terror in Ireland*, Paravision, London, 1971.

Marrinan, Patrick, *Ian Paisley: Man of Wrath*, Anvil

173

Books, Tralee, Ireland, 1973.

Northern Ireland Schools Examinations Council, *Certificate of Secondary Education, Rules and Schemes of Examination,* 1973-1974.

O'Brien, Conor Cruise, *States of Ireland,* Pantheon, New York, 1972.

O'Neill, Terence, *The Autobiography of Terence O'Neill,* Rupert Hart-Davis, London, 1972.

O'Sullivan, Michael, *Patriot Graves: Resistance in Ireland,* Follett, Chicago, 1972.

Paisley, Ian, *The Dagger of Treachery,* Puritan Printing Co., Belfast, 1972.

Paisley, Ian, *Northern Ireland: What Is the Real Situation?,* Bob Jones University Press, Greenville, S.C. 1970.

Presbyterian Church in Ireland, *The Northern Ireland Situation,* Belfast, 1972.

Riddell, Patrick, *Fire Over Ulster,* Hamish Hamilton, London, 1970.

Rose, Richard, *Governing Without Consensus,* Beacon Press, Boston, 1971.

Russell, James L., *Some Aspects of the Civic Education of Secondary Schoolboys in Northern Ireland,* N.I. Community Relations Comm., 1972.

Shearman, Dr. Hugh, *27 Myths About Ulster,* 1972, Ulster Unionist Party, Belfast.

Sheehy, Michael, *Is Ireland Dying? — Culture and the Church in Modern Ireland,* Taplinger, New York, 1969.

Smyth, Clifford, *The Axis Against Ulster,* Puritan Printing Company, Belfast, 1972.

Smyth, W. Martin, *The Battle for Northern Ireland,* Grand Orange Lodge of Belfast, 1972.

Streeter, Phillip, *Ireland's Hope,* Logos, Plainfield, New Jersey, 1973.

Study Group of the Institute for the Study of Conflict, *Ulster Debate,* The Bodley Head, London, 1972.

Target, G.W., *Unholy Smoke,* Eerdmans, Grand Rapids, 1969.

174

Ulster Unionist Patry, *Must This Go On in Ulster?*, Belfast, 1972.

Wallace, Martin, *Northern Ireland: 50 Years of Self Government*, David & Charles, Newton Abbot, England, 1971.

Ward, Conor K., *Western Religion: A Country by Country Sociological Inquiry* ("Ireland"), Mouton Publishers, The Hague, Holland, 1972.

Whyte, John, *Church and State in Modern Ireland*, Gill & MacMillan, Dublin, 1971.

III Periodicals

1973

"A Liberal's View of Ireland," William McMillan, *The Churchman*, Jan., 1973.

"Behind the Violence in Ulster," R.E. Hulbert, *Liberty*, Jan.-Feb., 1973.

"From Guns to Politics: White Paper on Ireland," J. Cooney, *Commonweal*, May 11, 1973.

"Ireland Between Two Walls," Avro Manhattan, *The Churchman*, March, 1973.

"Ireland: The Challenge of Change," T.P. O'Mahony, *America*, May 19, 1973.

"Irish Issue," *The New Humanist*, March 1973.

"Irish Stew," *National Review*, March 2, 1973.

"Northern Ireland: Murder and the Border Poll," Andrew Boyd, *Nation*, April 2, 1973.

"Reporter at Large" in the Finiston School, Belfast," Anthony Bailey, *The New Yorker*, October 29, 1973.

1972

"ABC's of Ireland's Endless Strife," *U.S. News*, July 31, 1972.

"After Derry and Newry," Anthony Howard, *New Republic*, Feb. 19, 1972.

"Agony of Ulster," J.E. Orr, *Christianity Today*, Nov. 10, 1972.

"Anglo-Irish Problem," Jack Lynch, *Foreign Affairs*, July, 1972.

"At School During Guerilla War," Dr. Morris Fraser, *Special Education*, June, 1972.

"Belfast Dialogue," Francis Russell, *National Review*, April 28, 1972.

"Billy Graham in Ireland," J.D. Douglas, *Christianity Today*, July 7, 1972.

"A City Divided", Bruce Cooper, *The Tablet* (*London*), January 22, 1972.

"Civil War Nobody Is Winning," J. Fromm, *U.S. News*, March 20, 1972.

"Ecumenical Efforts to Stem Violence in Ireland," *Christian Century*, Jan. 19, 1972.

"End of Stormont," Andrew Boyd, *Nation*, May 1, 1972.

"Impotence of the Churches," T. Beeson, *Christian Century*, Sept. 13, 1972

"Ireland: Religious War or Class Struggle?" M. Reik, *Saturday Review*, March 18, 1972.

"Ireland: The Killing Sickness," J. Breslin, *Nation*, March 27, 1972.

"The Irish Churches and the Credibility Gap," T.P. O'Mahony, *America*, Nov. 25, 1972.

"Irish Churches Appeal for Non-violence," *Christian Century*, April 26, 1972.

"Irish Sea of Troubles," G.H. Dunne, *America*, March 4, 1972.

"Letter from Ireland," J. Kramer, *New Yorker*, Feb. 19, 1972.

"Marching to Different Drummers," A. Roth, *Harpers*, April, 1972.

"The Myth and Truth of Irish Violence," Alfred McClung Lee, *Fellowship*, Sept., 1972.

"New Proposals for Ulster's Future," T. Beeson, *Christian Century*, Nov. 15, 1972.

"Nightmare of History," *Nation*, Dec. 25, 1972.

176

"Northern Island's Bloody Impasse," D. Reed, *Readers Digest*, Jan., 1972.

"Personal Reflections on the Strife in Northern Ireland," Michael Hamilton, *A.D.*, Sept., 1972.

"Protestants Who Live in a Ghetto of the Mind," John Whale, *London Sunday Times*, Jan. 30, 1972.

"Report from Northern Ireland," Norman Cousins, *World*, Nov. 12, 1972.

"Storm Over Stormont," J. Horgan, *Commonweal*, June 2, 1972.

"Trouble in Ireland," J. Horgan, *Commonweal*, Feb. 18, 1972.

"Ulster: Shadow and Substance," *America*, Aug. 19, 1972.

"Ulster's Point of No Return?" Donald Campion, *America*, March 4, 1972.

"When Irish Eyes Are Weeping," *National Review*, April 14, 1972.

1971

"A People Lost in Hate," Loudon Wainwright, *Life*, Aug. 20, 1971.

"Battle of the Boyne, J. Wyatt, *Commonweal*, April 23, 1971.

"British Vietnam," James Burnham, *National Review*, Aug. 24, 1971.

"Focus on Ireland, A Land Where Faith Matters," P. Elmen, *Christian Century*, Feb. 3, 1971.

"Gun-shy Investors Stay Away," *Business Week*, Dec. 4, 1971.

"Internal Affairs; Senator Kennedy's Suggestion That an American Statesman Act as Mediator," *Nation*, Dec. 27, 1971.

"Orange Bullies and British Tories," Andrew Boyd, *Nation*, April 26, 1971.

"Orange Enigma," *Christianity Today*, Aug. 6, 1971.

"Stormont on Britain's Back," Andrew Boyd, *Nation,*
Nov. 29, 1971.
"Ulster: A Kind of Plague," Andrew Boyd, *Nation,* Sept.
6, 1971.
"Ulster: The Children of Violence," *Newsweek,* April
19, 1971.
"Ulster: Must the Riots Go On Forever?" J. Laurence,
Catholic World, Oct., 1971.
"Ulster: Normally Abnormal," J.D. Douglas, *Christianity
Today,* June 18, 1971.
"Untangling the Irish Question," C. Kilcoyne, *America,*
Sept. 11, 1971.
"Vietnam on the Irish Sea," Anthony Lejeune, *National
Review,* Oct. 8, 1971.

1970

"Australia to Bar Paisley During Pope's Visit," *Christian
Century,* Oct. 28, 1970.
"Bloody Ulster: An Irishman's Lament," Brian Moore,
Atlantic, Sept., 1970.
"Divided Ireland: Continued Agony," J. Rockwell, *Chris-
tian Century,* May 13, 1970.
"Letter from Dublin," J. Kramer, *New Yorker,* July 25,
1970.
"Life in Belfast," J. Rockwell, *Christian Century,* Aug. 26,
1970.
"Ne Plus Ulster?" Andrew Boyd, *Nation,* July 20, 1970.
"Northern Ireland, London's Embarrassing Colony,"
Catherine Hughes, *Liguorian,* March, 1970.
"Paisley in Parliament," Andrew Boyd, *Nation,* May 11,
1970.
"Paisley's Progress," J.D. Douglas, *Christianity Today,*
May 8, 1970.
"Rebel in Armagh Jail, The Hater in the Pulpit," A.
Carthew, *New York Times Magazine,* Aug. 9, 1970.
"Religion and Politics in Northern Ireland," D. Clark,

TransAction, March, 1970.

"Ulster Revisited," Catherine Hughes, *America,* April 18, 1970.

"War in North Ireland," N. Moss, *New Republic,* Aug. 15, 1970.

"What's It Like in Belfast?" A. Cockburn, *Ramparts,* Oct., 1970.

1969

"At the Brink in Northern Ireland," J.A. Coulter, *Catholic World,* July, 1969.

"Belfast: In Glorious Remembrance," Carey McWilliams, *Nation,* Aug. 25, 1969.

"Bit of the Bogus," J.D. Douglas, *Christianity Today,* May 9, 1969.

"Bonfire in Ulster," N. Moss, *New Republic,* Sept. 6, 1969.

"Cameron Report on Ulster," *America,* Sept. 27, 1969.

"Case of Ireland," *Commonweal,* Sept. 26, 1969.

"Clearing a Political Slum," *Christianity Today,* Feb. 14, 1969.

"Coming Winter of Discontent," Andrew Boyd, *Nation,* Nov. 24, 1969.

"Confrontation, Irish Style," John Horgan, *The Critic,* Feb./March, 1969.

"Divided Ireland: Persistent Trauma," J. Rockwell, *Christian Centruy,* Nov. 19, 1969.

"Holy Wars," *Nation,* Sept. 8, 1969.

"Human Rights in Ulster," *Catholic World,* Oct., 1969.

"Ireland: Stage and Action," H.F. Woodhouse, *Christian Century,* Jan. 22, 1969.

"Ireland's Clash of Colors," R.W. Schleck, *America,* Sept. 6, 1969.

"Irish Ire," *Christian Century,* Aug. 27, 1969.

"John Bull's Other Island," J.D. Douglas, *Christianity Today,* Sept. 12, 1969.

"Northern Ireland: An Irish Protestant View," Norman

179

Porter, *Christian Heritage,* Oct., 1969.

"Not Defending the Indefensible," J.D. Douglas, *Christianity Today,* Oct. 24, 1969.

"Tensions Abate in Ulster," *America,* Oct. 4, 1969.

"Tragic Charade," C. Northcott, *Christian Century,* Oct. 1, 1969.

"Ulster After the Bludgeons," B. Kiely, *Nation,* May 19, 1969.

"Ulster Still on the Brink," T.E. Utley, *National Review,* Sept. 9, 1969.

"Ulster Under the Micro scope," J.D. Douglas, *Christianity Today,* Oct. 10, 1969.

"Ulster: The Gospel as a Club Raised," J.D. Douglas, *Christianity Today,* May 9, 1969.

1962-1968

"Catholics Take to the Streets," J. Horgan, *Commonweal,* Dec. 6, 1968.

"Ireland: Conflict in Ulster," H.F. Woodhouse, *Christian Century,* Nov. 27, 1968.

"Ireland: Paisley's Shabby Victory," J.D. Douglas, *Christianity Today,* Nov. 8, 1968.

"Pressure on Belfast Bigots," *America,* Nov. 30, 1968.

"Religious Strife Renewed in Northern Ireland," *Christian Century,* Oct. 23, 1968.

"Violence with a Religious Twist," *U.S. News,* Oct. 21, 1968.

"Another Hole in the Head," *Christian Century,* April 26, 1967.

"New Division in North Ireland," *America,* Nov. 25, 1967.

"Captain O'Neill and the Anti-Papist," J.H. Huizinga, *Reporter,* Oct. 20, 1966.

"Ecumenical Backlash in Belfast," E. McKiernan, *America,* July 9, 1966.

"Ireland's Hot Summer," D. Fisher, *Commonweal,* Sept. 2, 1966.

"Protestantism in the Land of St. Patrick," E. Best, *Christian Century*, Nov. 23, 1966.

"Unholy War of Preacher Paisley," H. Moffett, *Life*, Aug. 19, 1966.

"Northern Ireland: From Derry to Down," R.L. Conly, *National Geographic*, Aug., 1964.

"Catholics May Apply," *America*, March 23, 1963.

"Wearing of the Orange," Francis Canavan, *America*, Sept. 22, 1962.

IV   Newspapers

The *New York Times, Washington Post,* and *Christian Science Monitor* have all presented good, comprehensive coverage of events in Ulster. For depth of perception, background information, and the church-state angle, the *Monitor* stands far above any American publication. Peter Stuart and Jonathan Harsch have written superb articles on Ulster.

In England the *London Times, London Observer,* and the weekly *New Statesman* have been perceptive and illuminating.

In Ulster the *Ulster Protestant, Protestant Telegraph* and the *Bulwark* (published by Evangelical Protestant Society) present the ultra-Protestant viewpoint with great fervor. The *Belfast News Letter* is a moderate Protestant Unionist publication while the *Irish News* reflects Ulster Catholic opinion.

The evening daily, *Belfast Telgraph* is probably Ulster's best paper, moderate and judicious in tone and read by both sides.

"*Fortnight* is Ulster's liveliest, most discriminating publication. It is read by the small intellectual community and it is the most discerning and objective publication around.

Nusight and *Hibernia* are Irish Republic publications which report detailed commentary from Ulster.

V.   Bibliographic Essay

British government documents have the benefit of being "official" publications and are judicious, dispassionate, and detached in tone. They are also significant evaluations of government policy. The *Ulster Yearbook* is a factual, statistical almanac published annually.

The best all-round studies of the Ulster turmoil, giving the political, economic, and religious dimensions are Richard Rose's *Governing Without Consensus* and *Northern Ireland,* the *London Sunday Times'* journalistic analysis. Conor Cruise O'Brien's *States of Ireland* is especially useful for its perspective and the eminence of its author. The religious aspects of the crisis are covered comprehensively in Barritt and Carter's *The Northern Ireland Problem,* a very objective study; G.W. Target's *Unholy Smoke,* an angry and moving book; and Andrew Boyd's *Holy War In Belfast,* which surveys the ugly history of religious strife in Ulster. Max Hastings' *Barricades In Belfast* is an example of reporting at its best. Tony Gray's *The Orange Order* is a fascinating excursion into one of the world's most unusual societies.

Paul Blanshard's *The Irish and Catholic Power,* though written in 1953, is as relevant in much of its treatment of Irish church-state practices as if it had been written yesterday. Michael Sheehy's *Is Ireland Dying?* is a searching examination into the baneful and deleterious effects of certain Catholic policies on Ireland's cultural life, by an Irish intellectual.

Liam de Paor's *Divided Ulster* is one of the best historical summaries available. Garret Fitzgerald's *Towards a New Ireland* is an important examination of Ulster from the perspective of a government official in the Republic. The most significant of all books on Ulster is Morris Fraser's *Children in Conflict* because it probes the effect of religiously segregated education on interfaith relations.

Appendix

In contrast to the poems of heroism and pride expressed by Ulster's Orange Protestants appearing throughout this book, here are three typical Catholic songs which express unfavorable sentiments towards both the Protestants and the British. Most Catholic songs, like their poetry, extol their Gaelic heritage and express contempt for British colonialism. Only rarely do they attack Protestants as such.

Saint Patrick's Day will be jolly and gay
And we'll kick all the Protestants out of the way.
If that won't do, we'll cut them in two
And send them to hell with their red, white and blue.

Through the little streets of Belfast,
In the dark of early morn,
British soldiers came marauding,
Wrecking little homes with scorn,
Heedless of the crying children,
Dragging fathers from their beds,
Kicking sons while helpless mothers
Watched the blood pour from their heads.

I watched them spade the fragments in a bag
and look for more—
An eye, an ear — or if fate should be so kind.
A Limb yet in one place: Oh Lord:
Irelands tears run red with the Blood of her
own dear Children.
Irelands tears run red and the Tyrannts raise their
scornful head, and LAUGH:

I did not want to watch
Respect was thrown to the wind

A bag that held an Irish heart — a Head,
A Hand,
Oh Ireland wretched Land:

My eyes were loath to watch those spades
But my Heart —

My Irish Heart, Like those around cried
"Stay";
Stay and Hold your head erect for Irelands Son:

A British voice tainted with cold indifference
bid us go, No — NO
Firm we stood against their feeble threat
Although I did not want to see
I could not turn and Flee,
That would be an insult to Libertys Endeavour,

Dry your tears, Lift your Head,
COLM MURTAGH Died for IRELAND,
so Shall he LIVE FOREVER:
By Newry school girl.

This poem was written by a Catholic school girl and appeared in the pro-IRA *Republican News*. It apparently was written as the girl watched soldiers look for the remains of an IRA bomber who had accidently blown himself up. Her hatred for the British comes through loud and clear.

The Evangelical Protestant Society defends Ulster Protestants
in the three following editorials.

The Ulster Bulwark

OFFICIAL PUBLICATION OF THE EVANGELICAL PROTESTANT SOCIETY **Vol. 1, No. 7**

n. President:	Hon. Vice-President:	Hon. Treasurer:	Hon. Chairman:	Sec.:	Hon. London Rep.:
v. A. J. Finch, M.A.	Rev. D. Gillies, M.A.	Rev. F. S. Leahy	Mr. C. Brown	Mr. S. Milligan	Mr. D. Nash

DECEMBER  **1971**

COMMENT

ULSTER'S PRIDE.—Our little Province has been going through the fiery furnace of trials and tribulations. We are still the recipients of a ruthless campaign of murder and destruction. There are many who are seeking to destroy every fabric of our way of life. They seem to be possessed with a fanatical desire to bring our Province into a state of desolation. Many of the atrocities which they committed are devoid of human comprehension.

How then can you write about **ULSTER'S PRIDE?** What is there to be proud about in Ulster today?

We can still be proud Ulstermen and women in spite of the fork-tongued statements which are issued by the Roman Catholic Hierarchy in Ulster from time to time. The bishops have denounced the senseless violence, yet a Roman Catholic priest in Ardoyne has stated on Radio Eireann that the presence of I.R.A. gunmen can be justified in his parish. These gunmen, who just recently shot and killed in cold blood two members of the Royal Ulster Constabulary, one of whom was a Roman Catholic. A Roman Catholic monsignor attacks the I.R.A. from his pulpit and a Roman Catholic priest, speaking at an I.R.A. political meeting, urges the Eire Government to supply the I.R.A. with guns and so let them finish the job.

We are still proud, in spite of the provocation which has been hurled against the Protestant community unceasingly. It is a modern miracle to witness the restraint which is apparent amongst the Protestant majority in Ulster today. We are confident that no other community in the British Isles would have withstood the daily onslaught of the Republican bomber and murderer.

In spite of the ungodliness and wickedness of Protestants which is evident on certain occasions, nevertheless, there is in Protestantism a higher standard or morality taught than there is in Roman Catholicism and this must bear fruit some time in a community's life, and I believe that is now.

185

The Ulster Bulwark

OFFICIAL PUBLICATION OF THE EVANGELICAL PROTESTANT SOCIETY   Vol. 1, No. 5

Hon. President: Hon. Vice-President: Hon. Treasurer: Hon. Chairman: Sec.:   Hon. London Rep.:
Rev. A. J. Finch, M.A.   Rev. D. Gillies, M.A.   Rev. F. S. Leahy   Mr. C. Brown   Mr. S. Milligan   Mr. D. Nash

OCTOBER   Holy Bible   **1971**

COMMENT

BATTLEGROUND ULSTER.—It is sad to write again about the difficult situation in which we find ourselves in Northern Ireland. It is easy to talk about it, but when we try to explain what it is all about, it is then that we find difficulty.

Ulster, for many years, has been experiencing the Lord's blessing. From our little Province, which is similar in size to Yorkshire, there have gone more missionaries and preachers of the Gospel to many parts of the world than from any other country similar in size. Evangelical Christianity has been preserved and preached in a multitude of churches and other Christian gatherings. We have our missionary conventions and Bible conferences in great number and visiting preachers speak of the warmth of Ulster congregations.

What has happened to Ulster? Why is there so much killing and destroying? What prompts people to roam our streets at night with their bombs and bullets? Some very clever men can tell us about the days of the plantation, when English planters came to Ireland and lorded over the poor peasant people. But let us face realities. We are living in the twentieth century, but what have the Roman Catholics of Ulster been denied during the past fifty years? Perhaps what we should really ask is—What have they denied Ulster? When Ulster became independent from the south of Ireland, she did so because the **VAST MAJORITY** of her citizens wanted this to be so, and even today the same **VAST MAJORITY** want it to continue to be so. The Roman Catholics who were living in Ulster in those early days were given the option of either leaving Ulster or staying and living under the Union Jack. Many of those who decided to remain in Ulster failed to be loyal citizens of the Province and consequently there has been handed down from father to son a hatred of the British way of life which we have in Ulster. Therefore what many Roman Catholics have denied Ulster has been their loyalty. This denial has put a strain upon the method of government in Northern Ireland as it would be political suicide to entrust the powers of government to those who want to amalgamate us with a foreign state whose whole way of life is different from ours. They differ in language, in culture, and also in religion. This last difference is to us the most important one, for the laws of Eire, whether they be administered to Protestant or Roman Catholic, must be sanctioned by the Roman Catholic Hierarchy.

The majority in Ulster have their rights as well as the minority. We want to remain British, and we want to maintain our Protestant way of life, so that we want to hand down to our children the faith of our fathers which is based upon the written word of God. Is this a crime? Is this bigotry? Is this anti-Christian?

SEAMUS MILLIGAN.

186

The Republican gunman is the product of the totalitarian Church of me which has destroyed and killed in the name of God. Rome is winning England back ough the ecumenical movement—she is in many cases holding the balance of power in litics—she is condoning the gunmen of Ulster because she refuses to condemn them. We ve said it before and we will probably have to say it again—recognition of Rome as being Christian Church has inevitably brought God's judgment on the land. MAY THE GOD OF L GRACE BLESS US IN OUR HOUR OF NEED.   S. MILLIGAN.

In the summer of 1971 an Orange chaplain, Rev. S. E. Long gave this →
exposition of the Orange Order position.

"No Need to Apologise"

By S. E. LONG

ORANGEISM HAS SUFFERED from the all-embracing connotation which has been given to the word 'Orange' by mass media communicators in the press and on radio and television.

Reviled—revile not again!

Just as many of those who are loosely described as Protestants recognize no religious creed, so many who are labelled Orange have no connection whatever with the Orange Institution. They are not under any Orange society discipline. They have taken no Orange vows. They have no Orange conscience. They have other and different standards. They do not subscribe to the lofty **'Qualifications of an Orangeman'**, a document which breathes a spirit of piety, sympathy and generosity, to give a picture of Orangeism very different from that drawn by the vociferous critics of the movement which has not been particularly good at defending itself. The Institution has no delusions about itself. It does not claim to be better than it is. It resents the charges levelled against it of being guilty of ignorances, animosities and actions which it deplores no less strongly than do those other sensitive people who condemn social wrong thinking and wrong doing.

The Orange Order has no newspaper, no public relations officer, no pressing desire to publicize itself by the mass media of radio and television. Generally the Order speaks either by the Grand Master or the Grand Secretary. This method has the merit of ensuring that what is said by the Order has been carefully thought through before publication. When the Order speaks by handout to the media, as it does occasionally, it does so deliberately, after due consideration, generally effectively and always with a proper sensitivity of the need to speak only sense in any situation. Deliberative communications may lack the surprise, and the sparkle, of spontaneous utterances, but they are less likely to hurt a cause and more likely to contribute something of value to matters of community concern.

The Orange Institution has been singularly circumspect in its public utterances over the years. An examination of what it has said recently will prove the point. Such research could surprise the critic who often condemns thoughtlessly and without looking at the facts.

The public image of the Orange Order, with its efforts for peace in the turbulence through which the Province has passed, must be good when people become fairminded enough to acknowledge the case that the communicators often mean other people when they write and speak of guilty Orangemen.

Protestant—and proud of it !

The truth is that the Order, with its basis in Biblical Christianity and the Protestant tradition, has made a big contribution to the well-being of the country as self-respecting ordinary citizens and as people who hold influential and responsible positions in the country.

Orangemen have always had some things in common. First among them is their loyalty to the Protestant religion. This shows itself in their support of the churches to which they belong, and by their involvement as clergy, members of Select Vestries, Kirk Sessions and committees. The Institution has helped its members to jump over denominational hurdles, making it easy for them to share the worship of each other's churches and to understand something of the nuances of church principles and practices which have in them so much that is common and some things which are different. Joining together in the fellowship of the lodge helps Orangemen to know and to understand one another and to appreciate religious positions which have historical, doctrinal and utilitarian motivations to them. This praying together in private and public is a unity exercise which long pre-dates the modern emphasis on ecumenism which often has no greater involvement for the ecumenists than shared meetings for discussion and conversation of clergy and laity who have given little other evidence of any real desire for unity.

One thing Orange sharing has proved, while it is possible to think of a united Christian Church, it is nonsense to imagine a great Church in which there is uniformity of worship and church order. There has to be allowance made for the several attitudes, and responses, of Christian people in the practice of their religion. Variety is the spice of life. The cliche has merit religiously, too.

British—and true to it.

The second common ground for Northern Ireland Orangemen is their determination to maintain the British connection. The link has religious, political, economic and social overtones to it. There is a benefit of alliance which the Orangeman readily appreciates as a beneficiary but also as one who willingly contributes to the well-being of the shared and joined society. His Britishness is a regard of like for like.

There is much that is common in the Great Britain—Northern Ireland attitudes to life, liberty and the pursuit of happiness.

There is always the Ulster feeling that the association makes for safety religiously, there is no religious discrimination in Britain; economically, British financial help has been considerable; politically, in the sharing of like political ideals and socially, in the enjoyment of identical pleasures. Its position in the United Kingdom means so much to Northern Ireland that Orangemen, with their wholehearted devotion to the Province, are determined to ensure its continuance there. A closely integrated United Kingdom is something to be coveted by Ulstermen who feel as Orangemen do in the matter.

Whatever may be said to the contrary, the Orangeman is continually providing evidence of his continuing willingness to share with all other men of goodwill in the life of the community. He only asks that those who differ from him in their religious persuasions and political associations should be loyal to the state to which they belong by right of birth and citizenship. A man may say and do as he pleases within the law so long as he acknowledges this first demand on him. Every democratic state makes the same demand on its citizens.

We believe that Northern Ireland people who refuse this loyalty are deliberately blind to the advantages of citizenship in the United Kingdom. Their self-inflicted blindness is self-curable. May they work the cure to their advantage and ours.

$$\star \qquad \star \qquad \star$$

Discrimination—and How

FOR SEVEN OR EIGHT YEARS, and especially during the past eighteen months, the Protestants and Unionists of Ulster have been falsely accused and maligned generally by world-wide propaganda on TV, radio and the Press, with the result that those outside Ulster have been given the impression that the Roman Catholics of this Province are persecuted mercilessly—that they get no jobs, no houses, no votes; in fact, no say in anything. What annoyed the Protestant majority during this period was that the untrue allegations were not refuted immediately from official sources. It is only during the past year that a little has been done to counteract the false impressions given, perhaps in many cases too late, as they have already been absorbed. They should have been nailed with the truth as soon as they were made, and we hope that this will be done in future.

With the help of some Roman Catholics in Dungannon the Republican opposition hit on the subtle idea that because there is a majority of Protestants on or employed by a certain council or board, there is discrimination against Roman Catholics. Applying the same principle to local authorities in Great Britain, then almost every city and county there are guilty of discrimination. Then a mixture of anarchists, Republicans, Communists and others, who for years have wanted to present a bad impression of the Northern Ireland Unionist Government and the Protestant majority, found 'Civil Rights' to be a good label for this purpose. They commenced their campaign of marches, and violence started when they attacked the R.U.C. in the banned Duke Street in the city of Londonderry, and with it the world-wide publicity and false allegations.

The truth, of course, is that all the laws of Northern Ireland apply equally to all its people, irrespective of religion. Of all the Roman Catholics employed in Northern Ireland about 85-90 per cent. are employed by Protestants. In fact, the factories destroyed by Roman Catholics on the Falls Road and in Londonderry in which hundreds of their co-religionists were employed, were owned by Protestants. Contrary to some views held outside Ulster, there are Orangemen and other Protestants among the unemployed.

There are hundreds of Roman Catholics in the Northern Ireland Civil Service, especially in the Ministries of Agriculture and Health and Social Services. Since 1921 the Government kept open 33⅓ of the R.U.C. force for Roman Catholics. In hospitals under the care of the Northern Ireland Hospitals Authority the nursing and medical staffs comprise a large proportion of Roman Catholics, whereas in any hospital under Roman Catholic control the staff is 100 per cent. Roman Catholic.

In voluntary schools, the majority of which are Roman Catholic, 100 per cent. of salaries and 65 per cent. of building costs and national insurance contributions are paid by the 'bad' Protestant Government. The Church of Ireland, the Presbyterian Church or the Methodist Church has no separate teachers' training college, but have to share one college at Stranmillis with others, whereas the Roman Catholics have the privilege of having been provided with two—St. Joseph's for men and St. Mary's for women. Lord Craigavon made the offer that if a Roman Catholic farmer in Northern Ireland wished to exchange with a Protestant farmer in Eire he would assist them. There were applications from Southern farmers to come North, but no Roman Catholic applied for refuge in the Southern paradise. When a community is persecuted in any land, they flee the country and their population declines. In the case of Northern Ireland Roman Catholics are clamouring to enter and their population is increasing. Consequently, Protestants who pay most of the rates and taxes (partly because they are in the majority and partly because Roman Catholics, having bigger families, have more tax relief), pay most of the Roman Catholic maternity benefits, family allowances, education and university grants.

In Northern Ireland there are about 12,000 houses being built yearly, providing homes for people of all religions, and not only for Protestants as the subtle propagandists allege. In Gerry Fitt's constituency of West Belfast the Belfast Corporation, which has a Protestant majority, built about 650 houses in the Ballymurphy estate, where all but twenty are occupied by Roman Catholics, and nearly 1,000 houses in Turf Lodge estate, which is 100 per cent. Roman Catholic, and a separate parish has been formed of it. The Creggan estate in Londonderry is also largely Roman Catholic.

When the opposition parties speak about discrimination they do not mention Newry, which has a Roman Catholic majority on the Council; but no Protestant is employed in their offices or those of the Harbour Board, and very few on the outdoor staff or in the Gas Works. A similar situation exists regarding employment of Protestants and allocation of houses in Strabane and Ballycastle Rural which also have councils with a Roman Catholic majority. If the so-called Civil Rights movement was really interested in justice for all, they would also be making representations to these councils.

Ian Paisley's fortnightly journal, the *Protestant Telegraph*, expresses the unreconstructed, unrepentant view of thousands of Ulster Protestants. The following editorials and articles are from this paper.

SUBVERSIVE

ECUMENISTS

While events are fast escalating on the political and security fronts we dare not lose sight of the insidious inroads being made by the ecumenical movement to undermine our fundamental Protestant stand. Recent subversive moves that have been made include: The notorious Week of Prayer for Unity with Rome, when many so-called Protestant churches were subjected to the ravings of Rome's blaspheming "fathers."

Then there was the Interdenominational Conference in the Y.M.C.A., Dublin — Presbyterian, C. of I., Methodist, Salvation Army and papists. The Rev. Moran — minister of Abbey Presbyterian Church — revealed how he had aided the St. Vincent de Paul and Sisters of Charity. Then "Father" Valentine McLochlainn — Jesuit priest — addressed the gathering, led in prayer and pronounced the benediction.

On St. Patrick's Day at the infamous I.R.A. monument, the G.P.O. in Dublin (where the British Army wiped out the I.R.A. in 1916) there was an "ecumenical blessing of the Shamrock" by "Monsignor" Glennon, Rev. Salmon (Dean of Christ Church) and the Rev. E. R. Lindsay — head of the Methodist Church in Ireland. The parade past the G.P.O. included representatives of the I.R.A. thugs.

The most recent assault on Protestantism is being furthered by all the leading churches — including the Baptist and Congregational. The Gospel of St. Luke in a modern and modernist version is being distributed throughout the Province. The papists are getting their copies at the blasphemous mass. So called and supposed Evangelical Protestants are aiding the scheme — including the REV. MARTIN SMYTH, and REV. SAM WORKMAN.

The Gospel of Luke is in the "Today's English Version" — "Good News for Modern Man" version rather "False Views by Modernist Men" and is sponsored by the British and Foreign Bible Society which recently received a gift from the Vatican for its publishing endeavours. It must be stated that the T.E.V. rejects the cardinal doctrine of the Virgin Birth of the Lord Jesus Christ, it belittles the object of Christ's incarnation, it makes the day of our Lord's death a Friday — the "Good Friday" of Romish tradition.

For a further examination of the T.E.V. see "False Views by Modern Man" an exposure by Dr. Paisley. Price 15p (post paid) from Martyrs Memorial Publications, 356 Ravenhill Road, Belfast.

Ecumenism is a bad word in most of Ulster. Even such innocuous undertakings as an interfaith distributing of the Bible is roundly criticized by Paisley.

193

PROTESTANT MONEY TO HELP CHAPEL

So called Protestants have collected £600 to help St. Anthony's Roman Catholic Mass house to repair damage done in recent riots. Think of it Protestants paying to restore a Mass house to its former state!

Civil and religious liberty yes, but paying to restore idolatry and financing the facilities to perpetrate blasphemous rituals; subscribing to decorating confessionals for the unmarried "fathers" — NO!

"What fellowship hath light with darkness" — None. What a sorry tale; Protestants financing the stystem that has damned thousands to hell.

Riots in the winter of 1973 partially destroyed St. Anthony's Roman Catholic Church in East Belfast. A mob of several thousand Protestants burned the parish house to the ground and desecrated much of the church interior. A large number of Protestants were appalled at the behavior of their co-religionists and raised funds to help repair the church. The Paisleyites criticized this in the following vicious editorial. Apparently charity is not part of the Paisleyite value system.

194

SURPRISE
SURPRISE

A most surprising aspect of the recent elections is the meagre representation won by the much-vaunted Alliance Party. After reading the bally-hoo and the letters from members of its executive which daily appeared in the papers, one would have thought it would have swept the boards and romped home with an overwhelming majority. Instead, despite its publicity stunts, its boasting, its advertising, its placarding, its recruitment of Unionist defectors and its alleged finance from English sources, it has ended as an also ran. This seems to demonstrate that a party which is neither fish, fowl or good red herring has, in Protestant eyes, no place in Ulster, where one section yearns for a thirty-two pope's colony, and where the persecuted majority abhors the very thought of such a thing.

It is hard indeed to understand the mentality of anyone who would cast his vote for a middle of the road party in a country which is being systematically, surely and effectively reduced to ruins by popish rebels, against whom no effective counter measures are permitted to be used.

Nero is supposed to have fiddled when Rome was burning, and now Westminster idles whilst Rome burns Ulster!

This editorial represents the way militants feel about moderates in divided Ulster. It is difficult, often heroic, to be a moderate nonsectarian in today's Ulster. The Alliance Party's poor showing in the Regional Assembly elections shows this.

BY
APPOINTMENT

The scandal of Cabinet Ministers cavorting with prostitutes shocked the British public. Lords Jellicoe and Lambton had a particular interest in an Irish "call girl." This said person is a Roman Catholic with a strong republican background. Her family are devout papists, one uncle is a monk and an aunt is a convent nun. The low living of highly placed people is obviously a threat to security. But no alarm is apparent even though both Jellicoe and Lambton were Defence officials and their sleeping partner an Irish papist.

Papist immorality is always a factor, indeed in history there was a period called the "papist pornocracy" which rivalled the events of Sodom and Gomorrah. One must ask was this latest affair a delicate plot to discredit the British Government or to ascertain defence secrets in regard to Northern Ireland? Either suggestion has serious implications — will the British Government be alive to it or will British soldiers be dead by it?

The May 1973 scandal involving British Cabinet Ministers and call girls is given a new twist in this editorial.

Hitler's contempt for Protestantism

The past few years have given Ulster Protestants first-hand experience of how the Roman Catholic s y s t e m breeds Communism. In these days, as the Nazi I.R.A. Provisionals swagger around our capital city, we must also make ourselves cognisant of the links between the Roman Church and Fascism.

An interesting insight into this Papist/Fascist relationship is contained in a book called *Hitler Speaks,* by Hermann Rausching. This book documents the many interviews and conversations the author had with Hitler before the war.

Here are Hitler's own words on the subject of religion:

'I'm a Catholic. Certainly that was fated from the beginning, for only a Catholic knows the weakness of the Church. I know how to deal with these gentry. Bismarck was a fool. In other words, he was a Protestant. Protestants don't know what a Church is.

'The Catholic Church is a really big thing. Why, what an organisation! It's something to have lasted nearly two thousand years! We must learn from it. Astuteness a n d knowledge o f human nature are behind it. Catholic priests know where the shoe pinches.

'The Protestants haven't the faintest conception of a Church . . . They have neither a religion that they can take seriously nor a great position to defend like Rome.'

Here we see t h e nasty Nazi openly express his contempt for Protestantism and his admiration for the Roman system.

Printed and published by
The Puritan Printing Co. Ltd.
71 Ravenhill Road, Belfast

Catholics can't win. In one editorial they are accused of being an ally of Communism. Well, in this editorial, they are accused of being fascists.

In an attempt to duplicate the great SOLEMN COVENANT OF 1912, Protestant Loyalists devised the following covenant for Ulster's 1971 Jubilee.

IN DEFENCE OF NORTHERN IRELAND

Conscious of the forces at work for the overthrow of the Province and Parliament of Northern Ireland and convinced that any further interference in or undermining of the internal jurisdiction of the democratically elected government of Northern Ireland would be subversive of our civil and religious freedom and disastrous to our material well-being, we, whose names are underwritten, citizens of Northern Ireland, loyal subjects to Her Gracious Majesty Queen Elizabeth II, humbly relying on the God whom our fathers in days of stress and trial confidently trusted, do hereby pledge ourselves in solemn covenant throughout this our time of threatened calamity to stand by one another in defending our cherished position of citizenship in the United Kingdom and in using all lawful means to defeat any conspiracy to overthrow our Parliament.

In the event of the Constitution of Northern Ireland being suspended or abrogated against the will of the people, freely and democratically expressed for half a century, we further solemnly pledge ourselves, to work unremittingly for its complete restoration without tie or bond.

In sure confidence that God will defend the right, we hereto subscribe our names.

And further, we individually declare that we have not already signed this Covenant.

GOD SAVE THE QUEEN

Signed: _____

Here Paisley puts the blame of Ireland's troubles on the Church of Rome.

Rome's Policy In Ireland

In our last issue we published two items relative to public utterances by Roman Catholic priests. For reference we have brought a number of quotations and news items together to show quite clearly what Rome's policy is in Ireland.

THE POLICY

Cardinal Conway: "Bible Protestants and Rome have no common meeting place and never will have."

Professor. "Father" Coulter: "Northern Ireland is an unnatural organism conceived in deceit and maintained by force — Catholics hunger for the day when they will be united with the nation."

Dail M.P., MacBride: "All of us in the Government who are Catholics are bound to give obedience to the rulings of our Church."

"Father" Patrick MacCathmhaoil: "All the conditions required by moral philosophy and Roman Catholic theology for an armed insurrection were present in the North. The war being carried out by the Republican forces was endosed by the communities under seige."

"Father" Sean Gabriel McManus, brother of M.P. Frank McManus: "I want to state publicly and unequivocally that I am in sympathy with the I.R.A. Indeed sympathy is too weak a word."

A Liverpool priest on 'Panorama' said: "Every Irishman is a potential I.R.A. man."

THE STRATEGY

So we can see their policy quite clearly — they are opposed un-equivocally to the existence of Northern Ireland and to the position of the Protestants. How is their policy to be executed? :

"Father" Michael Connolly: "The I.R.A. campaign is not just a war, but a HOLY war against PAGANS." He called for support to be given to the I.R.A. and appealed to the Eire Government to "hand over guns which are going rusty, to the 'freedom fighters' in the North."

Jesuit priest Michael MacGriel, speaking of the use of the gun by the Roman Catholic and Fascist Provisional I.R.A. said: "In Ireland the gun is SACRAMENTAL."

"Father" Dominic Murray said on television last week that he would be slow to think that any of his parishioners would hand over an I.R.A. terrorist. He personally would not be a traitor to anyone.

A Holy war against pagans — that's how they describe it and the I.R.A. is to be the army to fulfill Rome's aspirations for a united Ireland.

THE POPE

The Pope in an address in the Vatican in September gave a vieled justification for the terrorists when he said that excessive military methods were being faced by Roman Catholic resistence. His words were re-echoed by the Irish Bishops who condemned the methods of the I.R.A. in delicate terms; but no condemnation of their IDEALS did we hear, rather they reverted to the ploy that political oppression was as bad as military oppression.

The Irish Bishops of the Church of Rome have threatened to excommunicate any known I.R.A. men from their Church but no excommunications have as yet been carried out.

True Protestants are in no doubt as to where Rome stands in relation to the I.R.A., and its campaign.

O. CROMWELL.

In early 1973 the Community Relations Commission completed (and then inexplicably supressed) a report on population displacement in Belfast since 1969. Sixty thousand people, or one out of every nine people in greater Belfast, were forced to move, to leave their homes, because of the tragic violence and fear. Eighty percent were Roman Catholics. The Paisleyites reject the report.

INTIMIDATION

An audacious and impudent suggestion is made in the published report of the Community Relations Commission. It is suggested that perhaps people should be asked to sign a declaration of community spirit! What an outrage! The members of the proposed Assembly are banned from taking an oath of allegiance to the Queen yet it is proposed to have an oath or bond of friendship with those who are patently disloyal.

The Community Relations document deals at length with intimidation and asserts that 80% of those forced out of their houses are Roman Catholics. The stage-managed evacuation of various areas by rebel elements has payed off with this Government sponsored propaganda. The rebels shunted families about Belfast and indeed throughout Ireland to refugee camps in the South. The press welcomed the tear-jerking emotional stories and the rebels kept up the momentum. To consolidate rebel support it was important to have enclaves of those of like mind — so Protestants were forced out and rebels shunted in.

The grossly inflated 80% intimidated papists will be highlighted and the Protestants blamed. One wonders have the authorities ignored the murderous intimidation against Protestants — in Ardoyne, where loyalist homes were burned out and Protestants murdered; Ligoniel where the entire village has been taken over by rebel hordes who now threaten the lower Ligoniel area; Lower Ormeau where the rebels have chased out the loyalists almost right down to the Lagan; Duncairn where only last week two Protestant families had to flee the clutches of rebel fire-raisers while the security forces looked on. Moyard and New Barnsley estates where no Protestants are allowed; Suffolk estate where constant bomb and gun attacks caused Protestant evacuation. There are many other examples in Belfast and beyond — like Lurgan.

It is not fashionable to consider the plight of Protestants, and this latest report would agree with that. The glare of publicity has gone to the rebels. The wreckers have been rewarded and by innuendo the Protestants blamed. If the Protestants were to blame — a proposition incidently that has absolutely no foundation — is there an equivalent zone to the butchery of Ardoyne? Is there a loyalist intimidation programme to rival that of Logoniel? Is there any comparison to the massive rebel takeover of whole estates like New Barnsley and Moyard? If the proposition were true there would be evidence of the effectiveness of Protestant action. There is none because there is no wholesale intimidation of Papists.

Propaganda has paid off for the rebels, but we know from experience that eventually they will bite the hand that is feeding them and then the truth will be apparent. Meantime NO SHAMEFUL PEACE TREATIES.

It must of course, be remembered that the Community Relations Commission was another act of appeasement and that the staff is almost entirely Roman Catholic — in fact even the notorious "Father" Marcellous was employed there until this newspaper revealed the facts and produced evidence of this.   O. CROMWELL.

The simplistic doctrinal compendium is often reproduced in the *Telegraph*, the *Ulster Protestant*, and other papers.

The Difference in a Nutshell

PROTESTANT CHURCH	ROMAN CATHOLIC CHURCH
Foundation: Christ the Rock.	Foundation: Peter (Cephas) — a stone.
Head: Jesus Christ.	Head: The Pope.
Mediator: Jesus only.	Mediators: Priests, Saints, Mary.
Means of Grace: Spiritual, Free.	Means of Grace: Material, Cash.
Mode of Worship: Spiritual.	Mode of Worship: Sensual, Material.
Its Guide: The Bible.	Its Guide: The "Church."
Its Aim: Salvation of Souls.	Its Aim: Wealth, power, political.
Object of Worship: God.	Objects of Worship: Images, Saints, Virgin Mary, Wafer God.
Governing Factor: Love.	Governing Factor: Fear, Superstition.
History: Light, Liberty.	History: Darkness, Slavery.
Secrecy: None.	Secrecy: Confessional, Convents, Jesuits.
Ministers: Merely Teachers.	Ministers: Indispensible priests.
Doctrine: Simple Gospel of Christ.	Doctrine: Mysterious, Pagan, Intricate.
Results: Peace, Prosperity.	Results: Strife, Poverty.
The End: To be with Christ.	The End: Purgatory — until released.

ONE OF THESE IS FALSE — WHICH?

The Paisleyites are critical of alleged liberal tendencies in Ulster's schools and colleges. They demand purity of thought. No dissent allowed.

Headmaster subverts pupils

In previous issues we have had cause to pinpoint the activities of the headmaster of the Methodist College, Belfast; and the invitation of such infamous personalities as John Hume, Rory McShane and 'Father' Tony Marcellus to address his pupils has been exposed and questioned.

A further incident has cast doubt upon the position of the headmaster in particular, and the school governors in particular. At their recent communal concert the National Anthem was deliberately omitted from the programme. It was pointed out to the headmaster—Mr. A. S. Worrall—that under the Public Entertainments Act the National Anthem must be played either immediately before or after the performance. At first he refused to discuss the matter, but eventually commented that the school did not sing *God Save the Queen* as it may be considered offensive to the Roman Catholic minority!

Worrall's friends

Not satisfied with bombarding his pupils with the philosophies of latter day rebels, Worrall has further embarked upon anti-monarchical and un-patriotic gestures, such as refusing to acknowledge Her Majesty. His subversion of innocent minds is of the most serious import.

Worrall's political friends are likewise suspect; together with Gerry Fitt (Republican Socialist) and Andrew Barr (Communist), he is a sponsor of the left-wing Northern Ireland Campaign for Peace in Vietnam; with such notables as Professor James Scott, pervert to Roman Catholicism; 'Father' Desmond Wilson, and Dr. Alfie Martin, he is a foundation member of the P.A.C.E. (Protestant and Catholic Encounter) organisation.

PACE is an offshoot of the New Ulster Movement, whose founder and self-appointed chairman, Brian Walker, is a personal friend of Worral; indeed, they both attend University Road Methodist Church.

So gathered round him Worrall has people whose comments, actions and reputations are well recognised as suspect by those who hold patriotism and sincere faith dearly. By disseminating 'liberal. 'community conscious' and ecumenical-political ideas through the organisations to which he belongs, inevitably he has an influence on youth; as a headmaster of the largest Grammar School in the British Isles, his influence is more intense.

An enquiry

The time has come for parents, parents' organisations, education committees and indeed the Ministry of Education to examine the political background of all teachers in Ulster schools. The consequence of anti-Protestant and anti-British ideas and ideals will breed a generation and emancipated electorate of young rebels. The actions of A. Stanley Worrall are worthy of an enquiry.

—COLLEGIAN

PROTESTANTS DUPED

The scene above is Oxford Street Bus Station a week after the mad bombers of the I.R.A. had devastated Belfast in a wave of 26 attacks. There on Bloody Friday six people were slaughtered and many more ·injured. The Unionist M.P. for North Down, Jim Kilfedder announced to the press that he was organising a memorial service at the Bus Depot, and various church representatives were to be invited. In fact the memorial services held at Oxford Street and Cavehill Road, the scene of another fatal bombing, turned out· to be ecumenical stunts.

Representatives of the Church of Rome participated in both services. Those so-called Protestant ministers who assisted the local agents of the Pope — the Antichrist — have deceived and mislead their congregations by recognising Popery as Christian.

Rome is behind the troubles — that is an indisputable fact; by inviting representatives to participate in a memorial service for the victims — all Protestants except for one — is adding insult to tragic injury. The papist Provisional I.R.A. has been shielded by the Roman Catholic community and by the priests of Rome.

Many Protestants attended the services to stand with those who had been bereaved. How did they feel when papist priests were brought along? In an atmosphere of mourning they were duped and deceived and they became party to ecumenical stunts. Protestants — to be worthy of the name — must shun the encroachments of the Church of Rome and should not by their presence or otherwise countenance any act or ceremony of popish worship — and that includes ecumenical services such as Oxford Street and Cavehill Road.

Paisley violently opposes interfaith prayer, worship or memorial serv ‘ ices.

Though the *Protestant Telegraph* theoretically represents only the Free Presbyterian Church of Ulster, it frequently meddles in the affairs of the Anglican Church. Paisley has led demonstrations in St. Paul's Cathedral in London, in the Anglican Church in Rome and Canterbury Cathedral to protest against the alleged Romanizing trends in the Church of England. Paisley has no jurisdiction whatsoever in the Anglican communion, but has become the self-annointed Cromwell of today.

Protestantism Betrayed

Anglicans and Roman Catholics have announced that they have reached a "substantial agreement" over the doctrine of the Mass.

Theologians of both faiths, have described the agreement as the most important statement since the Reformation." The Anglican and Roman Catholic International Commission of Bishops agreement hinges on Firstly the recognition of the "Eucharist as a memorial of the life, death and resurrection of Jesus Christ, and secondly that "the sacramental body and blood of the Saviour are *present* as an offering." The Commission says that "Christ's body and blood become really present and are really given."

What nonsense! The Thirty Nine Articles, which are to be undermined by this agreement, calls the Mass a "blasphemous fable and a dangerous deceit."

To suggest that the body and blood of Chrst are really and therefore bodily present is to say that the Eucharist is an act of Cannibalism.

The Church of Rome claims to continue the act which the Scriptures say was completed nearly 2,000 years ago. We cannot regard it as anything other than a deception, a mockery, and an abomination before God. The so-called sacrifice in the Mass certainly is NOT identical with that on Calvary, regardless of what the priests may say.

Irrespective of what the Commission says, Evangelical Protestants stand by the Bible — no popery — we will not go a-massing!

O. CROMWELL.

The Protestant Question Box

ROMAN PERSECUTIONS

Has the Church of Rome been able to convince the people by reasonable argument to accept her peculiar teaching?

No. She has constantly used intimidation and persecution in order to hold her own or to stop the spread of "heresy", as Protestantism is called.

Give an illustration of the ruthlessness of Romanism?

The Bartholomew Massacre, 1572, when in one night between 50,000 and 70,000 Protestants were butchered in Paris.

Who was responsible for this?

It was a plot organised by the Queen Mother, Catherine de Medici, and the Jesuits.

How were the Roman Catholics instructed to carry out the massacre?

They were instructed by the priests at Mass to put a light in the window and wear a band with a cross on the right arm and also one round the head.

What was to be the sign of the attack?

The tolling of the cathedral bell in Paris at 12 o'clock on the eve of the feast of St. Bartholomew, 1572.

How were the Protestants kept in ignorance?

The Roman Catholics were instructed by their priests to keep the matter strictly secret.

Has this sort of thing happened more than once?

Yes. There have been several butcheries of Protestants. In 1641, more than 40,000 Protestants were massacred in Ireland. In the same period thousands of Coventanters stained the hills of Scotland with their blood.

The Question Box of the *Ulster Protestant* keeps the past vividly alive.

Strong opposition to the British entry into the Common Market has been expressed on several occasions by Ulster Protestants, because of the alleged Roman Catholic dominance of the Market. Note in one editorial the fear of a Continental Sunday. Ulster is still a rigidly sabbatarian society where almost everything closes on Sunday by law or social pressure.

NO! to Common Market

The Prime Minister says he appointed Robin Bailie to head the Ministry of Commerce because he is a pro-Marketeer. Our television screens have been showing scenes of violence—not in our own country, but in Brussels—when the Common Market agricultural policy was opposed by thousands of disgruntled farmers. Riots leading to the death of two people highlighted the fact that the E.E.C. cannot equitably organise policy for the member countries. There is nothing in the Common Market to commend it to the United Kingdom; we would lose existing trade agreements with Commonwealth countries; lose our political sovereignty; lose our Royal House; lose our legal system; lose our liberty and freedom to a Council of Ministers who would dictate our way of life. The threat of a Continental Sunday is just one aspect of life under the Treaty of Rome.

Tell your M.P. at Stormont and at Westminster that you do not want Rome Rule; we reject the Common Market and all that it represents.

NO! to Common Market

PAPAL DIPLOMATIC ACTIVITY

Despite persistent claims that the Pope desires to be rid of the trappings of temporal power—for example, t h e Vatican army has now been disbanded—the claim to temporal authority is as emphatic as ever.

Pope Paul h a s n o w appointed a diplomatic representative to the Common Market.

Papal diplomatic activity has a strange and sordid history. In recent decades it includes the attempt to come to terms with the Communist regime in Russia from 1917 to 1928; the 1929 pact with the Fascist dictator Mussolini; the support of General Franco i n h i s rebellion against Republican Spain, which led to the complete suppression of religious liberty for 30 years; the Concordat with Hitler in 1933; and the notorious Concordat with Colombia, S. America, under which, to this day, Protestant missionary activity is banned in two thirds of that country's territory.

BRITAIN'S MINISTER AT THE VATICAN

The appointment of a Minister to the Vatican cannot but make us ask anew: Why should Britain have any representation at the pocket-sized State of the Vatican? It is quite clear that the Vatican's political power would be non-existent if it rested merely on the Pope's temporal sovereignty over the Vatican territory. It rests rather on the Pope's headship of the Roman Catholic Church and his blasphemous claim to be the Vicar of Christ. The less Britain has to do with 'the Man of sin and the Son of perdition' the better for herself.

These editorials express opposition to the maintenance of a British ambassador to the Vatican. Britain inaugurated diplomatic representation at the Vatican during World War I. However, Britain maintains only a Minister at the Vatican rather than a full fledged ambassador; the Vatican sends an Apostolic Delegate to Britain rather than a Papal Nuncio. Of course, many responsible Protestants, Catholics, and Humanists oppose diplomatic relations with the Papacy.

When Pope Paul was considering a visit to Britain for the opening of the new Liverpool Cathedral, Paisley issued this rejoinder and even called the Pope "His Satanic Majesty."

Pope for Britain?

Although Vatican sources have been keen to deny it, there is increasing speculation that his Satanic Majesty, Pope Paul VI, is to visit Britain and Ireland, perhaps later this year. It has been argued that a Papal tour would help to increase confidence and respect in the hierarchy, which has received quite a bashing with such controversial matters as celibacy, the Mass and contraception.

In the Irish Republic there has been a large-scale defection from t h e Church to Socialism in its various Communist species. A visit from the Pope would result no doubt in a right-wing Papist move along fascist lines.

This year is t h e 800th anniversary of Henry II's invasion of Ireland, with Pope Adrian IV's blessing. The subjugation of Ireland to 'widen the bounds of the Church' was both bloody and fierce; any attempt to celebrate the fact with the Pope's presence would result in similar barbarity.

It must be said that there is an element in the British Isles who would resist any visit of the Pope. Mere vocal opposition would be futile. The Pope must not be permitted by the Government or the people to desecrate these sceptered isles.

St. Patrick forever

The Church of R o m e organised an open air mass at Hyde Park to celebrate St. Patrick's Day. It is lamentable that the vast majority of Protestants are ignorant of St. Patrick's Protestantism; yes, St. Patrick was no emissary of the Pope. Presbyterian historian, Rev. Dr. T. Hamilton, writes of Ireland's patron saint:

'The whole story of the Romish origin of Patrick's labours is a pure fiction. Besides, his teaching was very far removed indeed from Romanism. Romanism glorifies the Virgin Mary; there is no trace of Mariolatry in any of Patrick's writings. The Church of Rome puts our blessed Lord into a very subordinate place; with Patrick, Christ is all in all. The Bible receives but little honour from Rome; Patrick knew it well himself, and looked to it as the supreme standard of truth . . . The impudence of any attempt to make out Patrick to have been a Romanist is only equalled by its futility. His whole spirit and teaching and aims were not only not Rome's, but were as different from hers as possible . . . Patrick's writings were undeniably and conspicuously Protestant; distinctly Trinitarian and thoroughly evangelical.'

One of the traditional historic debates between Protestants and Catholics in all of Ireland revolves around the real religious views of St. Patrick, Ireland's patron Saint. Both sides claim him as their own.

211

WAS
FAULKNER
AT MASS?

There is a report circulating that Mr. Brian
Faulkner, the redundant Premier, attended a
Mass at Dromore, County Down, on Monday,

7th August last. Faulkner, the man who banned Orange processions, and the annual parade in Dungiven and declared Armistice Day parades illegal, apparently went to the Mass and made all the responses. "Brother" Faulkner, the redoubtable Orangeman that he is, has as yet not denied or answered the press report that highlighted this infamous act. If the report were untrue one would expect a denial and an apology from the publisher. If the report were true then we expect the Grand Orange Lodge of Ireland to act accordingly and sling out someone who has blatantly violated the laws of the Institution

There is and can be no justification for any Orangeman to attend the blasphemous and unchristian Mass.

This article glorifies a rumor about where the Prime Minister attended church one Sunday. The Orange Order prohibits its members from attending a Roman Catholic service for any reason whatsoever. A Unionist member of Parliament was expelled from the Order for refusing to be disciplined by the Order for attending a Catholic service in his constituency. Another prominent Orangeman, Sir Robin Finahan, was expelled from the Order because he attended his niece's wedding in a Catholic Church in Dublin!

The unfortunate intervention of Sen. Kennedy into the Ulster debate prompted this reply.

6 PROTESTANT TELEGRAPH 5-2-1972

KENNEDY

We are all aware of the sentiments held by Senator Kennedy with reference to Northern Ireland. He is a real "chip of the oul block" and no friend of either Westminster or Stormont — especially the latter — and has been well tutored by the Papal propaganda machine. Indeed, he may be regarded as being part of it, and his recital of the so-called grievances of the rebels here is indeed impressive. However, conditions in his own country are far from being imaginary, and excerpts from a magazine printed in America — the land of the free — reveal an atrocious state of affairs beside which the most outlandish lies of Irish Papists fade into insignificence. The city of Newark in New Jersey is cited as an example of racial discrimination and social atrophy. In 1967 some 40,000 unemployed negroes in the city rose *en masse*, and in a week a large area of Newark lay in blackened ruins, the cost of the destruction being approximately eighteen million dollars, twenty six people had died and well over one thousand injured, whilst fourteen hundred were arrested. Much of the property destroyed was never rebuilt and lies to this day as a token of the policy of the white Americans towards the negro population. That which has and is taking place in Newark can very well be repeated in other urban areas where discontent and justifiable resentment

214

against discrimination is rampant. Why does not Senator Kennedy advocate the intervention of the U.N.O. in this situation, the authenticity of which is beyond question? Why does he endeavour to interfere in the internal matters of the United Kingdom, which have been mis-represented and lied about until any Loyalist resident here cannot believe that he is actually existing in the midst of such injustice? The "Alice in Wonderland" atmosphere of the propaganda machine cannot gull the native Northerner, and Kennedy and his American associates would be much better to examine their own country, where *genuine* grievances of the minority are superabundant. A writer in another American magazine says that he "would like to see Kennedy and his fellow thinkers be required to live for one year in down-town Washington or the slums of New York City, or the central district of Seattle, *without a gun.*" In such lamentable circumstances common throughout the United States, one is reasonable in supposing that the attention of Kennedy would be absorbed in eradicating same, and leaving Northern Ireland to eliminate the gunmen in the only permanent way.

Despite ferverant claims of loyalty, Protestant loyalty to Britain is conditional, as the following editorial indicates.

"HONOUR THE QUEEN"

The Protestants of Ulster have clung to the British connection mainly because they see in it the security for their Faith and the future of the Reformed Church in their beloved North. This belief in England has been based on the supposition that the Constitution is fundamentally Protestant — Ichabod — and so allergic to Popish influence. But, the very loyalty of Orangemen is essentially conditional, and their love for the British Crown is bounded by two words — "Being Protestant." Notwithstanding the faithless acts and downright betrayal by the British Government and politicians the Orangeman still regards the Crown as his semper *idem,* the unchanging symbol of a Protestant succession and the bulwark against Papist guile and Papist violence. How far this trust can be justified is certainly a matter for argument and eventually for demonstration. Assuredly, should the propaganda machine succeed in its purpose, and should the English time-servers have their way, and we are consigned to the Hades of a Dublin Government, our only crime being that we cling to legislative union with the United Kingdom, the name of Westminster shall stink in the nostrils of every free Protestant in this world.

Roman Catholics formed defense committees in their neighborhoods after internment was introduced. Here is a typical wall poster. ➡

216

SPECIAL BULLETIN

A meeting was held today in St. James's Social Club between the local Defence Committee, residents of St. James's and district and the local Sinn Fein Cumann together with The Womens Action Committee of the area.

A Central Committee was formed and the following decisions were made: —

1 To pay no rent, gas or electricity bills.

2 Anyone found to be non-co-operative will be severly dealt with.

3 Anyone found breaking and entering or looting will be dealt with, with extreme penalty.

4 Any shopkeepers found to be over-charging will have his premises closed.

5 Anyone obstructing a Central or street committee man, or fraternising with the enemy will be severly dealt with.

6 Street gangs will be formed to empty bins and burn rubbish to assist residents during the present emergency.

7 We urge people of the area to give a good audible alarm signal when British Raiding Parties enter, example — rattle bin-lids, sound car horns, whistle etc.

8 We appeal to parents to keep children off the streets during the hours of darkness.

This policy will be maintained until all internees are released.

Join the Republican Movement and help to defeat British agression against the Irish people.

This article seems to indicate that the Paisleyites would welcome the destruction of Roman Catholic Churches.

IN BRIEF . . .

'DEE
CHAPEL

After the chapel in Donaghadee had been bombed (propably another accident) the local minister — following in Donald Gillies' footsteps, raced down to the Mass-house to convey his regrets to the local agent of the Roman dictator and antichrist (according to West-minster Confession of faith). The Rev. Beggs, the Presbyterian minister in question waffled on about the plight of his brother "Christian." My Bible and my Faith teach me that the worship of Rome is anti-Christ and the Mass is a blasphemy and a sin before God. Can we, if we are honest to the Master, regret that a temple of Baal has been overthrown?

Pope Paul's public statements on Ulster have been curiously ambivalent. He indicated that there would never be peace in Ulster until Roman Catholics were treated justly. This could have been interpreted (and was by the following editorial) as a blessing to the continuance of Catholic opposition to the Ulster government.

PAPA'S PLEA

The Papal Antichrist, as the Westminster Confession calls him, issued his regular dose of rubbish in St. Peter's Square, the other Sunday. He moaned on about Ireland — Mary's Dowry — and cried about the denial of rights to Roman Catholics in Ulster. To add insult to injury he said that the Roman Catholics had been provoked to violence — which was against their nature!

Papa Paul must be going senile — "against their nature;" has he forgotten his own involvement with that product of popery — Adolf Hitler; his position in regard to Mussolini and the Fascists; his attitude to Franco? Did not his predecessors sanction and bless the Home Rule Movement, Sinn Feinn, and the I.R.A.? Did Pope Benedict not bless and commend the rebels in 1916 at the Easter Revolution? The hands of the Roman Catholic Church are continually being steeped in the blood of sainted martyrs. From before the Reformation until today the Roman Catholic Church has been involved in political intrigue and terror. Her aim has been the extermination of Bible Protestantism, and that aim has not changed. She has used many guises — fascism, nazism, socialism, liberalism and now ecumenism to suppress, by foul means, a Protestant Witness.

Bible Protestants like Luther of old must stand up and be counted before the enemy comes in like a flood, with Papa Paul on the crest of a wave.

Paisley will attack the British Royal Family when they fail to hew to the strict Protestant lines, despite his protestations of loyalty to the Crown.

Princess Margaret Visits Roman Catholic Shrine

Recently Princess Margaret visited the Roman Catholic Church and Shrine of St. Boniface, Crediton, Devon. She was received at St. Boniface's by the Vicar-General of Plymouth Diocese, Mgr. Patrick J. Tobin, and the parish priest, "Father" George Hay. She also attended a united service in a park at which there were a large number of Roman Catholics. On the day preceeding her visit there was a united procession of Roman Catholic, Anglican, Methodist and Congregationalists who all took part in a short service at the Roman Catholic Shrine.

COMMENT— Joshua called upon the people of his day "To choose ye this day whom ye will serve." He set them an example by adding that "he and his house would serve the Lord." If only we had such leadership today — what a difference it would make to our nation, for undoubtedly God will never honour a nation that condones idolatry.

BOYCOTT

Last year an effective campaign was carried on by Loyalists to boycott Eire goods. This campaign has slackened off slightly, so we appeal to all Loyalists to be extra vigilant. Those who are known to be supporting enemies of the State should likewise be treated.

**BUY BRITISH
SUPPORT PROTESTANT
SHOPS
BOYCOTT EIRE GOODS**

— BRITISH LOYALIST COMMITTEE —

Including L.O.I.E. (Action Committee), Murray Club Apprentice Boys of Derry (Liverpool Branch), British Constitution Defence Committee (Liverpool)

DEMONSTRATE

IN LONDON IN SUPPORT OF ULSTER on

SATURDAY, 29th APRIL, 1972.

ASSEMBLE HYDE PARK CORNER AT 1 p.m.

STAND BY ULSTER IN HER HOUR OF CRISIS

The situation in Ulster has encouraged sympathizers to demonstrate for the Protestant Cause.

The Protestant Independent Party

(P.I.P. Leader and Founder The Revd. Harry Wharton, 1959 Just returned from Spain)

WILL PLACE A

Candidate to Fight in North Ayrshire Constituency—

(SCOTLAND)

FOR THE GENERAL ELECTION

IF YOU WILL GIVE IMMEDIATE FINANCIAL SUPPORT?

We are strongly opposed to the Common Market and Treaty of Rome.

Your Protestant Freedom is in Peril!

Defend it with all your might—and your money is necessary—NOW!

Please mail your Gifts To-day for Election Campaign expenses to:

REV. HARRY WHARTON,

c/o Mr. Ken Donnan,

80 Boglemart Street,

Stevenston, Ayrshire

SCOTLAND (Election Campaign Address)

All Cheques and Postal Orders made out in favour of Rev. H. Wharton
Tel.: No.:
STEVENSTON 61276

All Donations Acknowledged

The following are selections from books, advertisements, and other miscellaneous items which give a flavor of the militance of many → Ulster Protestants.

222

BOOKS
EVERYONE SHOULD READ

E.P.S. BOOKROOM

ROOM 59, 26 HOWARD STREET, BELFAST BT1 6PD, NORTHERN IRELAND

BOOK LIST AND ORDER FORM

BOOK LIST No. 2

Title	Author	Price inc. Postage
Personal Evangelism—John R. W. Stott		7p
Five English Reformers—J. C. Ryle		30p
Jesus Christ Super Star—Or Saviour and Lord— Pastor John Coleman, a critique of the Rock Opera		15p
Miracles—Healing — Henry Frost		36p
("I strongly recommend this most valuable study" —D. M. Lloyd-Jones)		
The Believer at and After Death— Bishop D. A. Thompson		21p
The Papacy—Its History and Dogmas— Leopold D. E. Smith		18p
How to Read the Bible—C. H. Spurgeon		13p
The Reformation Catechism—Bishop Poynet		16p
Leading Roman Catholics to Christ (Irish Edition)		35p
Foxes Book of Martyrs		28p
The True Catholic Faith (bound volume of our Christian Correspondence Course)		30p
Occultism (The origin of Mormonism)		45p
The Church of God (Booklet for Roman Catholics)		5p
The True Church and The False		7p
More about the Mormons		5p
Public Enemy No. 1—Who is He?		12p
According to Matthew Henry		12p
2 Booklets on Armstrongism		13p
The Dark Arts in Bible Light		29p
The Church of Rome and The Lord's Day		7p
A Cross on The Lord's Table		8p
"Ulster Protestant"		6p
The Catholic Bible has the Answer		5p
When Real Life Began		4p
Roman Catholic New Testament		62p
Ronald Knox Translation)		
Christian Workers New Testament (with Psalms) (Soft back)		68p
(De Luxe Edition)		£1.55
The Challenge of The Reformation		15p
Spurgeons Catechism		9p
Series on Reformers—Calvin, Cromwell, etc		15p ea.
Instruction in Christianity—A study of Calvin's "Institutes"		69p
Roman Slaves—by an ex-Nun		9p

Please send the following books:

INDEX

227

Hamilton, Canon Michael 16, 44
Heath, Prime Minister Edward 38, 39
History of Religious Conflict in Ireland 27-40
Home rule battles 29-30

Ireland (Irish Republic) abortion 105-106, adoptions 102, anti-clericalism 118-119, birth control 104-105, censorship 93, 110-118, constitutional provisions on religious liberty 93, 102-103, education 106-110, mixed marriage problem 100, Protestant community in 94-100
Irish News 17, 181
Irish Northern Aid Committee 134-136
Irish Republican Army (IRA) 38, 39, 40

Kennedy, Senator Edward M. 38, 141-154

Manhattan, Avro 45-46
McManus, Father Sean 45, 136

National Association for Irish Freedom 135-140
Northern Ireland Labour Party 22

O'Brien, Conor Cruise 45, 99
O'Neill, Terence 11, 32, 35, 36, 87-88, 125
Orange Order 34, 35, 63-67

PACE 128
Paisley, Ian 19-20, 35, 52-53, 55-62
Parker, Rev. Joseph 127
Patterson, Monica 129
Political parties, divided by religion 19-25
Pope Paul VI, statements on Ulster 51-52
Protestant Telegraph 52-53, 57, 62, appendix

Reconciliation, organizations working for 126-129
Religion, role in Irish history 27-40, in Ulster state schools 74-85
Religious statistics 11, 12, 26, 100
Republican Party (Irish) 23

Separatism in education 69-90, 106-110
Smyth, Rev. Martin 42, 124
Social Democratic & Labour Party (SDLP) 22-23, 37
Social status of Protestants and Roman Catholics 14
Solemn Covenant of 1912 30
Special Powers Act 31

Unionist Party 19

Vanguard Movement 20, 21
Vatican, involvement in Ulster crisis 51-52

Weir, Rev. Jack 50
White Paper 34, 39-40
Whitelaw, William 33, 38
"Witness for Peace" 127
"Women Together" 40, 129

228